They Call Me
Eddie Morrison

They Call Me
Eddie Morrison
Cherokee National Treasure

Bill Keith

Foreword by Principal Chief Bill John Baker

PELICAN PUBLISHING COMPANY
GRETNA 2016

Library of Congress Cataloging-in-Publication Data

Names: Keith, Bill, 1934- author. | Morrison, Eddie, 1946-
Title: They call me Eddie Morrison : Cherokee National Treasure / Bill Keith; Foreword by Bill John Baker.
Description: Gretna : Pelican Publishing Company, 2016. | Includes bibliographical references.
Identifiers: LCCN 2016011776| ISBN 9781455622245 (hardcover : alk. paper) | ISBN 9781455622252 (e-book)
Subjects: LCSH: Morrison, Eddie, 1946- | Sculptors—United States—Biography. | Cherokee artists—Biography. | Morrison, Eddie, 1946—Themes, motives.
Classification: LCC NB237.M66 K45 2016 | DDC 730.92—dc23
LC record available at http://lccn.loc.gov/2016011776

All photographs by Eddie Morrison unless otherwise noted

Printed in China

Published by Pelican Publishing Company, Inc.
1000 Burmaster Street, Gretna, Louisiana 70053

Contents

Foreword

Eddie Morrison is a credit to Cherokees everywhere, and all of us marvel at his beautiful work. He is, indeed, a Cherokee National Treasure. But as you read through the pages of his dramatic life's story, you will see that he is also a man of vision and great courage. His magnificent work is anchored in Cherokee culture and the very best of Cherokee tradition. Today he stands beside other great artists—both past and present—who, through their works, have preserved our history.

People throughout the land know Eddie as a man of great compassion who has created works of art that represent the Cherokee people with pride. Through his art, Eddie helps us remember who we are and who we were, and his work brings our legends and traditions to life.

Eddie grew up in Tahlequah, Oklahoma, full of hopes and dreams and a deep sense of destiny.

They Call Me Eddie Morrison: Cherokee National Treasure tells the story of his elderly grandmother Jane Batt Brackett—a full-blood Cherokee—who raised him and instilled in him the values he cherishes today. She had such a tremendous influence on his life, and he repeatedly pays tribute to her in the pages of this book.

The story also takes you behind the scenes of his life and work and his dreams for the Cherokee people, giving you a glimpse of what the man Eddie Morrison is really like. For instance, he says, "My life has evolved over time with so many different and magnificent events and I am thankful every day for the wonderful world of art that has opened so many doors for me. I consider myself abundantly blessed among men. This is what I was born to do."

His desire to keep the Cherokee culture and history alive is closely tied to all those who came before him. He says, "We walk in the footprints of those who came before us and we must remember that they were our ancestors and deserve our respect. I sometimes feel that their spirits are with us and what we do reflects in them and where they came from. I think they would be proud that we Cherokees have risen from the ashes of defeat and near-destruction to become the great Cherokee Nation we are today."

As you read through the pages of this book, you will laugh and you will cry, but you will never forget the courage that took Eddie from small beginnings to a place of national honor. And his story will become a model for Cherokee young people, encouraging them to believe that they, too, can climb the mountain to success. Eddie teaches us that.

Although his work is displayed at the Smithsonian and the Department of the Interior in Washington—and in galleries and private collections all across this land—his success has changed him not at all. He is still a man of great humility.

Eddie says that Will Rogers is one of his heroes, for he was a man who was always proud of his Cherokee heritage. Rogers once declared, "If you want to be successful, it's just this simple. Know what you are doing. Love what you are doing. And believe in what you are doing."

Eddie, like Will Rogers, has discovered that pathway to success.

In 2014, it was my great privilege, on behalf of the Cherokee Nation, to honor Eddie as a Cherokee National Treasure. With this well-deserved distinction, he now joins other great Cherokee artists who were instrumental in keeping the Cherokee heritage and culture alive.

Eddie, we Cherokees are more than 300,000 strong, and on behalf of all of them, let me say "thank you" for the light you have brought into our hearts.

Bill John Baker, Principal Chief, the Cherokee Indian Nation

Introduction

Eddie Morrison is an ordinary man who has lived an extraordinary life. He is a proud son of the Cherokee Indian Nation who rose from small beginnings to become one of America's best-known Native American artists.

When he looks back on his career, he realizes it was like riding on a carousel with ups and downs, victories and defeats, and he never knew for sure when the music would fade away.

Eddie traveled a long and winding road in pursuit of his profession and his dreams of success, and today, he has a heart full of thanks that his dreams have come true. His works of art are displayed in the halls of some of the most prestigious museums in America—including in the National Museum of the American Indian in the Smithsonian and in the Department of the Interior, both in Washington, D.C.—as well as famous galleries. His work is also displayed in galleries and private collections in foreign lands.

Eddie believes that the sum total of his life is far more than being a successful painter or sculptor. His heart beats with love for his family and the Cherokee people, whose legacy and culture he wants to preserve through his art. He has worked diligently for decades to do his part to keep that legacy and culture alive. He constantly beats the drum for a future filled with hope and promise for the Cherokee people and all Native Americans.

Eddie has a deep passion and strong philosophical convictions concerning his work. Besides his own feelings and interpretations of art forms, his ideas and themes come from the philosophies of his Indian ancestors. He draws on their beliefs about respect for life—all that is around us—and the great Creator.

Although he has become more successful than he could ever have imagined, he is a man of great humility and has no desire to be a celebrity. Rather, he prefers living a quiet life with his wife, Faye, at his country home and studio in Steely Hollow, only a few miles from Tahlequah in northeastern Oklahoma.

Eddie says, "Art tells a lot about us to future generations. I like to think that some of my art will be here on this earth hundreds of years after I'm gone." However, he appears somewhat uncomfortable when talking about his success. He would rather focus on the form and substance of his work. "About my work, I consider the natural forms of the wood and stone and believe in letting the materials speak for themselves. They have their own stories to tell. An old artist once told me, 'If you have a real story to tell in your piece, it will make it interesting.'"

Eddie is convinced that art is a passion within a person, a gift from the Creator that will never go away.

Writing *They Call Me Eddie Morrison*: *Cherokee National Treasure* was a delightful adventure that I enjoyed immensely. Although I had heard good things about Eddie, I never really knew the true measure of the man or the magic in his work.

But what is Eddie Morrison really like? I spent hours interviewing him and Faye in their storybook log home near Tahlequah, Oklahoma. I also talked with his children, brother and sister, friends, colleagues, and the directors and owners of various art galleries where his work is displayed.

Getting to know all these people—and spending time with them—was a grand experience.

After those several months and deep reflection on the man and his work, I've learned that Eddie is a man of compassion, which colors everything he does in his personal life and his work. I am also convinced he will continue to keep the proud Cherokee heritage alive through his art.

Thank you, Eddie, for a job well done. Your amazing works of art will forever echo in our hearts. The thousands of us in the United States and foreign lands who love your art are thankful that you have shared your great passion and unique gift with all of us through your magnificent paintings, carvings, and sculptures.

This is Eddie Morrison's story. I enjoyed writing it, and now may you, the reader, enjoy the journey as you share his great adventure with him.

They Call Me
Eddie Morrison

Chapter One

Cherokee National Treasure

Eddie Morrison knew that it was going to be a night to remember—for a long, long time. He had often wondered what it would be like. Throughout his life, he had felt as though he were riding a whirlwind. But he knew that tonight his odyssey would be complete, when he would be named Cherokee National Treasure, the highest honor the Cherokee Nation gives to its sons and daughters. Yes, this was the night his wonderful dream would come true. Yet, it seemed like a fairytale.

"It's still like a dream," he told his wife, Faye, as he drove away from their log home on a hill down to Steely Hollow Road. She smiled as he turned south on Highway 10, which follows the rippling, turquoise waters of the Illinois River, its picturesque shoreline stretching for miles.[1]

The sun had almost disappeared beyond the mountain in the west, but they could still see great boulders, nature's giant sentinels, hovering over the highway and the river nearby. When they reached Sparrow Hawk Mountain, Eddie accelerated for the drive up its face. He steered past the precipitous ravines below and the legendary Lover's Leap, high on a bluff overlooking the river. The spot is named for the story of two lovers who jumped to their eternity when their parents would not allow them to marry.

A slight smile creased his face as he squeezed Faye's hand. Questions raced through his mind. "Will I be nervous? Will my family and friends be proud of me? Will I get all choked up? Why am I already nervous on the greatest night of my life?"

For the past several days, the events in his life had seemed surreal. At times he had to stop and remind himself that his life was about to change in a wonderful way.

The scenario began when the phone rang early on a Monday morning a few weeks before. Faye checked the caller ID and saw that the principal chief of the Cherokee Nation was calling. She had a feeling that it was important.[2]

She picked up the phone. "Hello, and good morning."

"Good morning, Faye, this is Bill John Baker. Can I speak to Eddie?"

"Sure, Chief, hold on just a minute." She had a premonition why the chief was calling and hoped in her heart it was the news that she had yearned to hear for several years.

Faye handed the phone to Eddie, who was sitting at the breakfast table drinking a cup of coffee. "It's Chief Baker. He wants to speak to you."

Eddie took the phone. "Hello, Chief, how are you this morning?"

"Fine, Eddie. I have some good news for you."

"Okay, I always like good news."

"Well, this is really good news. The Cherokee Nation has named you a Cherokee National Treasure."

Each year, the Cherokee Nation selects certain Cherokee citizens, who have shown exceptional knowledge of Cherokee art and culture, to be named Cherokee National Treasures. The award was created in 1988, and since then, more than eighty Cherokees have been so honored. Qualifying Cherokee citizens have made important contributions to the preservation of craft-making, language, graphic arts, contemporary arts, and music. "Being recognized as a Cherokee National Treasure for doing something I love has been an amazing experience," said Tommy Wildcat, who received the award in 2013 for his river-cane flute music. "It says a lot about our tribe that they really appreciate the people who are keeping our traditional ways alive."

The news overwhelmed Eddie. At first, he didn't know what to say, but he felt he had to say something. After all, he was talking to the principal chief of the Cherokee Nation, the largest Indian tribe in America.

The federal government—by treaty and by law—recognizes the Cherokee Nation as a sovereign nation. The Cherokee people chose Principal Chief Bill John Baker and Deputy Chief Joe Crittenden in a national election. The seat of tribal government is the W. W. Keeler Complex near Tahlequah, Cherokee County, Oklahoma, the capital of the Cherokee Nation. With more than 330,000 citizens, it is the largest tribal nation in the United States. The Cherokee National Holiday has been celebrated each year since 1953 and commemorates the signing of the 1839 Cherokee Constitution. A large annual festival in Oklahoma, attracting nearly 100,000 visitors from around the world, features entertainment and cultural and athletic events.

At last, Eddie found his voice. "Thank you, Chief, I'm honored and hope that I deserve the award."[3]

"You well deserve the award, Eddie. You are a tribute to Cherokee people everywhere."

The chief explained there was to be an awards banquet at the Sequoyah High School gymnasium, and he would send those details.

"It's going to be a great celebration, Eddie, and we are all proud of you. Goodbye."

Eddie hung up the phone and turned to Faye. "Cherokee National Treasure! They're going to honor me as a Cherokee National Treasure!"

Faye didn't know whether to cry, shout, or dance. She explained it like this: "At first I was all choked up with emotion, for I knew it was such a great honor and I was so proud for Eddie. Then I hugged and kissed him and danced all over the house."[4]

Through the years, she had stood by her husband as he had received all kinds of awards and recognition. "But this was his highest honor and he was deserving. He had worked so hard in his art for so many years."

Now the big night was here. After a twenty-minute drive from home, they arrived at the Sequoyah High School's multimillion-dollar gymnasium.

Eddie opened the car door for Faye. As they walked hand in hand into the banquet, he felt as though he were walking on pins and needles. People were laughing and talking and having a good time. He saw dozens of friends who had come to share the great honor with him and with the others who were to receive the award. He and Faye made their way to his reserved table, where friends and family were waiting. He had invited several to join him. Dr. Isabel Baker, his high-school speech teacher, gave him a big smile and told him how proud of him she was. Longtime friend Jimmy Locke shook his hand and introduced his friend Diane Gates. Buddy McCarty and wife Diana were there from Owasso, Oklahoma, to share in the celebration.

Donna Tinnin, director of the Cherokee Art Center in Tahlequah, congratulated him. Cherokee Tribal Councilor Victoria Vasquez, also a Cherokee artist and recipient of the award, was there to see Eddie receive the National Treasure honor. Also in attendance were his aunt Fannie May Duffield and cousin Dolly Richardson. He gave them a big hug.[5]

As they sat at the banquet table laughing and talking and waiting for dinner to be served, Eddie was overwhelmed at the thought of receiving the award. His past thirty-eight years as a Cherokee painter and sculptor played through his mind like an old silent movie, telling the story of what brought him to this place, at this time.

The movie showed days of anguish and days of hope, good times and bad, mountains high and valleys low. He saw himself traveling halfway across the United States in his old pickup truck to art shows, with very little money but a burning passion to show and sell his work. Sometimes he sold only one or two pieces—or none.

He grinned when he remembered the long days on the road and the sleepless nights in the bed of his truck under a camper shell.

Now, surrounded by friends and family, he felt a deep sense of gratitude to everyone who helped him to this point in his life. It was a night that would live forever in his heart.

As his mind wandered back to his boyhood, his heart filled with thanks for his full-blood Cherokee grandmother Jane Batt Brackett, who had taken good care of him and to whom he owed so much. How he wished she could be here to share this moment with him. She would be so proud. So would his mentor Allan Houser, the renowned Chiricahua Apache Indian artisan known as the "Michelangelo of America," this country's preeminent Native American sculptor who was and forever would be his hero.

His journey into the past also brought mental images of all the art dealers and collectors who believed in him and featured his works in their galleries across America. He thought too of the people in foreign countries—Japan, England, Russia, Ireland, Canada, Israel, Australia, and perhaps places unknown—who purchased his art and took it to their homelands.

Eddie hoped it wasn't all a dream, but if it was, he didn't want to awaken. For he was about to be named a Cherokee National Treasure.

He sighed and said to his friends, "I wish they would just go ahead and give the awards. This waiting is too much for me."

Cherokee Tribal Councilor Joe Byrd, master of ceremonies, at last walked to the podium, picked up the microphone, and welcomed all the guests. He introduced Chief Bill John Baker, Deputy Chief Joe Crittenden, and several members of the tribal council. The ceremony began, and soon he said, "Our next Cherokee National Treasure award goes to—Eddie Morrison."

Eddie froze. His mouth felt dry, and he thought his knees would buckle. Holding back tears, he managed to make his way to the platform, where Chief Baker waited. The crowd shouted, clapped their hands, and rose to their feet in a standing ovation. Eddie, a little embarrassed at the applause, had a sheepish grin on his face. He felt a tremendous sense of pride in his work, his family, and Cherokee people everywhere. But soon that pride was tempered by a deep sense of humility.

Chief Baker presented the award. He noted that Eddie—and three others who received awards—exemplified the values important to the Cherokee people. "All of these honorees deserve our deepest respect and gratitude. We are proud our National Treasures are getting the exposure they deserve. They preserve our traditions and educate people so that the spirit and the heritage of the Cherokee Nation remains as vibrant today as it ever was."

The chief placed the National Treasure medallion around Eddie's neck, shook hands with him, and presented him with a plaque. Once again, the crowd roared its approval.

Eddie prepared a speech for the event but didn't have the opportunity to present it. So he posted it online. It came right from his heart. Here's what he posted:

> What an honor! I had a speech prepared, but remembered my speech teacher from high school Isabel Baker would be here. I know she will be sitting out there taking notes to give me a grade, so I decided to keep it short.
>
> Let me say thank you to our Creator for the blessing. Thank you Chief Baker and the Cherokee Nation for this honor. Thank you to Mrs. Baker for nominating me. Thanks to my great friends that wrote letters of recommendation: Victoria Mitchell-Vasquez, Donna Tinnin, Susan Pourian, Mike Daniel. Thank you to my wife Faye and my children and family.
>
> Faye said I still have to mow the lawn, but could wear my beret.
>
> Thanks to all my friends here tonight. We are blessed to be Cherokee. Thanks to my ancestors whose spirits I know are here looking on proudly.
>
> As I walk in the footprints of those that came before us, I'm very humbled. God bless the Cherokee Nation.

After the ceremony, Faye said, "Eddie was just glowing."

Wiping away tears, she was pleased that so many of his friends were there to honor him. "Dozens crowded around Eddie wanting their pictures taken with him to remember the wonderful occasion."

Just as Eddie had predicted, it was a night to remember, and he knew he would carry it, along with all of his family and friends, in his heart forever.

Chapter Two

The Early Years

Margaret Morrison knew it was time. She hurried to the Indian Hospital in Claremore, Oklahoma, where her baby was to be born. She gave birth to a boy and she called him Eddie Morrison. The date was September 29, 1946. A few days later, she returned home to Tahlequah, where the baby would live with his brothers and sisters.

Tahlequah, the oldest city in Oklahoma, is located in the foothills of the Ozark Mountains near Tenkiller Reservoir. When the Cherokees arrived in the 1800s in what was then known as Indian Territory, they established a tribal government and built educational institutions. Tahlequah and nearby Park Hill soon became vital Cherokee centers. Later Tahlequah would become the capital of the Cherokee Indian Nation, as it remains today.

Eddie doesn't remember much about his early days, but when he was still very young, something happened that he wishes he could forget. That was the night the cops raided their house. His mother had married J.T. Hummingbird two years earlier. They were bootleggers and sold whiskey. At that time, it was illegal to sell any kind of beer or whiskey in Oklahoma.

One night everything was quiet around the home. Margaret and J.T. were listening to the radio. The children were getting ready for bed.

Suddenly there was a loud knock on the front door, and the excitement began. Eddie remembers it as if it were yesterday. "I was about five years old and we were living on Oak Street. Several Tahlequah cops knocked on the front door and one of them shouted, 'We know you're selling whiskey and we're here to take the whiskey and you're going to jail!'"

Margaret was startled. This was not supposed to happen. She regularly paid local police officers for protection so that she could sell the whiskey. "Mom said they told her if she paid the right people, the police would never bother her, and she had paid them a lot of money," Eddie explained. Now the police were knocking on her front door. It made her mad. She opened the door and didn't say anything. Eddie notes that was really something for Margaret, for she always could come up with a few choice words.

Several police officers, wearing cowboy hats and gun belts with big pistols in large brown holsters, pushed open the door and walked into the house. Eddie thought they looked just like some of the pictures he had seen in the funny books that J.T. had bought for him and the other children.

The policemen couldn't find the whiskey, and Eddie's mother and J.T. wouldn't tell them where it was. Eddie said it was a scary night for him and his brothers and sisters as they watched the cops searching through the house. "It was like the cops and robbers in the movies we would go see at the Sequoyah Theater on Muskogee Avenue in Tahlequah, where Mom would take us on Saturdays."

There had never been that much excitement in their home, and Eddie—in wide-eyed awe of the policemen—followed them all around the house. "They looked everywhere, turned over mattresses in the bedroom, searched the pantry, looked in the attic, and even went outside and looked under the house but found nothing. All the time, my mom was trying to quiet us kids and telling the cops to get out of her house. J.T wasn't saying anything, just smoking one cigarette after another."

Then a strange thing happened, something no one would ever have expected. As the policemen were getting ready to leave, one of them looked down at Eddie. "Do you know where the whiskey is?"

Eddie peered up at the big policeman and thought he looked like the giant in one of his picture books. Then he remembered that his mother always told him to tell the truth. "It's in the back bedroom."[1]

"Come on and show us," the big policeman said.

They followed Eddie to the back bedroom, where he pointed up in the closet. His mother and J.T. had cut out a section and made a false ceiling. Eddie had watched them hide their whiskey up there many times.

The policemen found the whiskey in the false ceiling and loaded it in boxes. Then they handcuffed J.T. and hauled him off to jail.

Margaret was fuming and couldn't believe their rotten luck. Her son had given them away. They charged J.T. with bootlegging. A few days later, a district judge sentenced him to six months in the local jail. But for some reason, the judge had mercy on Margaret and dismissed the charges against her.

Eddie never could figure out why they didn't jail his mother. She was selling the whiskey right along with J.T. "I guess the judge knew she had all of us kids to look after."

Something else added to the drama in their home that night. Margaret wondered who had squealed on her to the police. The police ripped her off even though she was paying for protection. But she couldn't tell the judge that she had bribed the police. She could go to jail just for that. So she kept it to herself. She really didn't want any more trouble with the police. She figured that something must have gone wrong, or perhaps she was paying the wrong people. One day Eddie heard her ask herself, "Don't they know I was just trying to make a living in hard times?"

Years later, Eddie learned that some of the most prominent men in Tahlequah bought whiskey from her and J.T. "She often thought they should have tried to help her since they liked her whiskey so much. But not one of them lifted a finger to help her and acted like they didn't know my mom and never heard of her or J.T."[2]

Even though he was just five years old, Eddie remembers going with his mother to visit J.T. in the old county jail across the street from the county courthouse in Tahlequah. "It was an exciting time for a kid. Visiting the old stone jail brought back stories of cops and robbers I had read about in funny books."

Sometimes, for reasons unknown, the jailor wouldn't let them see J.T. So they would go around the side of the jail, where Margaret would lift Eddie up and he would hand J.T. a pack of cigarettes through the steel bars. Eddie says J.T. always appreciated the cigarettes and never blamed Eddie for his going to jail.

Even today, Eddie has vivid memories of that fateful night when the police busted his stepdad and hauled him off. "Years later, the family would joke about how I ratted out my mom and stepdad to the cops that night."

Eddie's mother often told him the story of how they brought the illegal liquor into Oklahoma. One night she and J.T. were driving through Seneca, Missouri, a couple of hours away from Tahlequah, with a carload of whiskey. The Missouri State Police almost caught them at a highway roadblock.[3]

When Eddie first heard the story, he thought it was like an adventure right out of a cops-and-robbers movie. "Mom explained that when they saw the police roadblock, they knew the state troopers were searching cars for illegal whiskey and they sure didn't want to get caught. So they pulled into a gas station to buy some gas and watch the troopers as they searched the cars. Then, out of the clear blue sky, J.T. saw they were checking only every third car."

Margaret told Eddie that J.T. came up with a strategy for getting through the roadblock. She said, "J.T.'s plan sounded pretty good to me because I didn't want to get caught and spend the next year in jail for running whiskey. So he watched for his chance and pulled in behind the third car in line, and the troopers motioned us on through. We drove far into the night to get to Tahlequah, where several men had parked their cars and were waiting on the street near the house, anxious for us to arrive."[4]

His family had an outlaw side, but Eddie said they were never mean or violent. "Although it's no excuse, times were rough back then, and in those days folks did a lot of things to try to make a living."

There were also some moonshiners in the family who made their own whiskey. "It's not something I'm proud of, but it did help them survive. I never did learn where they hid their stills—maybe up Highway 10 in Black Fox Hollow or somewhere back along the pig trails in the Cookson Hills, where no one, including the law, could ever find them. From time to time, country folks living in the hills would hear an explosion when a moonshine still would blow up. It's usually caused when explosive alcohol vapor escapes and is ignited. People all over the area could hear the explosion."

•••

Although it didn't dawn on him back when he was just a boy, later Eddie learned an important lesson that sometimes bad things work for good in people's lives. "J.T. getting arrested and going to jail changed all of our lives. When he got out, he decided to stop selling whiskey, go straight, and get a real job. He applied to a trade school in Muskogee, Oklahoma, about thirty miles from Tahlequah, to learn to become a welder and was accepted."

After J.T. completed his training and was certified as a welder, he discovered that the United States government was helping Indians around the country find jobs and relocate to other states. The government found him a position as a welder at the Savannah River Plant in South Carolina, which included five reactors. It was built in the early 1950s during the Cold War to produce materials for nuclear weapons. He and Margaret loaded Eddie and the six other children in their old, worn-out Ford and drove 1,400 miles from Tahlequah to Barnwell, South Carolina, to begin their new lives.

Eddie still remembers the long trip. "J.T. pulled a homemade trailer behind the old Ford. He had made it out of a truck bed and it only had two tires. Mom filled the trailer with clothes and a few pieces of furniture. But a bearing kept going out on one of the wheels and we would be stuck for several hours beside the road until J.T. could get it fixed."

They finally made it to Barnwell, and Eddie's sister Nancy Hummingbird remembers that it was a boomtown because of all the work at the atomic-energy plant. "Housing was scarce, so all Dad could find for us was a small trailer. We moved in and Dad went to work at the plant."

The trailer proved to be way too small for the seven young children—Don, Carolyn, Richard, Kenneth, Eddie, Nancy, and Jesse. But Nancy said that their mother found a place for all of them, even though some of them slept on pallets on the floor.[5]

They later moved into a house in Blackville—about ten miles from Barnwell—where they were not so crowded.

Nancy remembers that eventually the family moved to Tennessee. "We lived in Tennessee, but Dad worked on a dam on a Tennessee Valley Authority project and traveled back and forth on weekends to see Mom and us children."

Nancy described their parents. "Mom and Dad were total opposites. Though both were Indians, she had a hot temper and Dad was very reserved and didn't have a whole lot to say. Mother took good care of us. She was only five feet, two inches tall but she made sure no one mistreated any of us, and if they did, they would answer to her."

Nancy was just a baby when they moved to Barnwell, but when she grew older, she and the other children had a lot of fun. "We played tag, kick the can, hide and seek . . . and at night we would catch lightning bugs in a bottle."

Sometimes their mother would let them watch television, and Nancy said they really enjoyed children's programs. "We watched *Howdy Doody, Captain Kangaroo,* and *Lassie.* The boys really liked *Sky King* and *Roy Rogers.*"[6]

Margaret enrolled the children in school in Barnwell, but Eddie remembers that things didn't go very well for him. "I was six years old when I entered the first grade. On the first day of school, a group of white kids formed a circle around me and beat me up because I was an Indian. My teacher stood by and watched but did nothing."

Eddie told his mother and J.T. what the kids had done, but neither seemed particularly concerned. "They didn't even volunteer to go to the school to talk to my teacher about what happened. They just told me I had to stand up for myself."

Those were difficult days for Eddie, for he didn't understand racial discrimination and why the kids at school wanted to fight him. "I was the darkest one in our family, and in the summertime I turned almost black. Racism was rampant in South Carolina toward Indians and any other people of color—even among the children."

Because he was so dark, the Barnwell School Board had a special meeting to discuss whether to send him to the school for colored kids or keep him in the all-white school. "They debated the issue for some time. . . . But they finally decided to let me stay in the white school."

The bullying by the white kids had a profound effect on him. "I started having a lot of emotional problems because of the way they were treating me. Once again my mom told me, 'Eddie, you've got to fight back.' But I was just a little guy, six years old and small for my age. I didn't know how to fight, and several of them would jump on me at the same time."

Even when he was older and looked back on the way he was treated in the Barnwell school, he never could understand the hatred toward him and his family just because they were Indians and had dark skins. "I can understand why someone might not like another person because of something they might do or say but not just because of the color of a person's skin."

Sometimes when the family would go to a restaurant, the waiters would not serve them and told them to leave. "My half-brother Jesse is five years younger than me. When he was just a little boy, I [took] him to the barbershop to get a haircut. The barber wouldn't even acknowledge we were there but just looked at us and said nothing. We continued to wait not knowing what to do. The barber would take the other boys who came in after us and cut their hair. Finally he looked down at us and said, 'I don't cut Indians' hair.'"

It was terribly embarrassing for the young Indian boy from Oklahoma. "I remember how ashamed I felt and sad. But I'm glad that at that time Jesse was too young to understand what was going on and why the barber said what he did to us."

Something else troubled Eddie about living there. "They wouldn't let my brothers and me swim in the public swimming pools with the white kids. I never could understand why we were called the *n* word when we were Indians. They even had separate toilets with *Colored* written above one door and *Whites Only* over another. And, of course, we had to use the one for the coloreds."

One night, the Ku Klux Klan burned a cross in their front yard in Blackville. "These men in scary white robes and white hoods hammered on the front door and ordered J.T. and Mom to get the family and get out of town. That made my mom mad. She stomped out the front door carrying a double-barreled shotgun and pointed it right at the men in the robes. Then she gave them a good cussin', for she could cuss like a sailor. She told them if they didn't get out of her yard and take the cross with them, she was going to blow a bunch of holes in the bedsheets they were wearing. The Klansmen couldn't wait to get out of our yard and out of range of Mom's shotgun."[7]

Eddie remembers the night he took his little brother, Jesse, skinny dipping in a swamp near their home when his brother was only three years old. "We didn't know anyone was around, but a woman saw us and called our mom. She told her, 'Your boys are out there in the swamp naked as jaybirds and there are skeeters and snakes and gators and everything else out there.' Mom came after us and she was mad. She told us to get out of the swamp and get our clothes on and get home. When we got there, she tanned our hides, and we never went skinny dipping in the swamp again."

An especially sad event during those painful days greatly affected him. "My mother's sister committed suicide. We all returned to Tahlequah for the funeral. I sat there looking at her casket and couldn't imagine why she would do such a thing and take her own life. 'Perhaps no one will ever know,' I thought."

Today Eddie believes there was one bright spot in his life in South Carolina, and for that he said he will always be thankful. "The elementary-school library had a collection of Little Blue Books for children that tell the stories of great men like Daniel Boone, Davy Crockett, Benjamin Franklin, presidents, and great explorers. I read all of them and the men became my heroes. For long and precious hours, I was free from my miserable existence as I lost myself in the lives of great heroes."

During the long and hot South Carolina nights, Eddie often lay awake and dreamed of faraway, exotic places where there was a dragon to slay or a mountain to climb. He also dreamed of being like some of the men he read about in the Little Blue Books.

According to Eddie, the books all focused on how the subjects overcame difficulties as kids and became great men. "Those books really helped me. It's funny how books will do that to you. I could identify with the [subjects] and it would just transform me. When I grew older and had my own children—Jennifer, Monica, and Ron—I always encouraged them to read."[8]

Eddie's brother Jesse, who also became a renowned Indian artisan and now lives in Bisbee, Arizona, remembers an incident that took place years later when the family was driving across Louisiana. "They also had separate drinking fountains for whites and coloreds. Our mother, Margaret, walked over to a white water fountain to get a drink. A white man standing nearby said, 'Why are you drinking out of that fountain? That fountain is for white folks only.' Mom didn't say anything, just glared at the man and walked away."[9]

Jesse was just eight months old when they lived in the trailer in Barnwell. Since there was so little room, Margaret spread a blanket for him in the kitchen sink, where he slept.

Although Jesse is the youngest of the children, he has a lot of memories of growing up in the Deep South. Times were difficult for the whole family, and South Carolina was a different world from Tahlequah. "It was a strain on all of us seven children at first living in a two-bedroom home there in Barnwell. We all seemed happy, at least at home. But, of course, Eddie was having a lot of trouble at school."[10]

Jesse remembers his father with affection. "Dad was really a good-looking guy, a handsome Indian who looked like the image on the Indian-head nickel."

Although his father was a hard worker, Jesse says he left the discipline in the family to Margaret. She was able to manage seven children and make sure they were wearing clean clothes when they went to school. She spent a lot of time taking care of them. "She was the one who made us mind and stepped in when some of us got into arguments and fights. Dad just never got involved in those kinds of things. He had a quiet presence, very quiet, but there was also an authority about him that all of us respected. He made a lot of good money working at the plant, but there were seven of us children to take care of."[11]

Jesse continued, "Dad worked at the atomic-energy plant and later at the massive Tennessee Valley Authority, building dams as part of a flood-control program on the Tennessee River. He was really a brave man. One day on the job, one of the other workers was about to be crushed by a huge crane, and Dad climbed a high ladder to save him. He was very strong and excelled in sports, especially at the Sequoyah Training School and at Bacone College in Muskogee."

Later in life, Jesse saw some pictures of his father. "He served in the army during World War II and in a military honor guard. He really looked sharp in his chrome helmet and white leggings, standing at attention holding his rifle. I was so proud of him."

Jesse remembers that while they were living in South Carolina, his brother Kenny had a terrible automobile accident. His father did his best to help him recover. "At night, I could hear Kenny crying when Dad was giving him physical therapy. I give Dad a lot of credit for helping Kenny like he did. But Kenny also had severe brain damage and was paralyzed the rest of his life. He died years later in Tulsa, Oklahoma, when he was only forty-three years old."

But Jesse also has the sad memory of his father being killed in a construction accident in 1972, while working on a Tennessee River dam near Brownsville, Alabama. "He was welding and the weld came back on him. Some gas and bad air exploded and killed him. Mom and Eddie and I went to Brownsville and claimed the body. The Reed-Culver Funeral Home in Tahlequah sent an airplane to pick him up, and I flew back in the plane with my dad."

Through the years, Eddie has tried to block out the painful memories of his childhood in the South. He knows that his sad experiences at the hands of the white children in the Barnwell school had a profound effect on him even years later. "I've gone through my whole life being shy because of the way I was treated. All through grade school and high school, I was afraid of what someone might say or do to me. I couldn't even get up in front of a group to speak without having a panic attack."

Eddie never adjusted to the schools in South Carolina. So when he was in the fifth grade, his mother and J.T. thought it would be best for him to return to Tahlequah to live with his grandmother Jane. All the other children would stay with them.

When they arrived in Tahlequah, Eddie told his mother and brothers and sisters goodbye and carried his few belongings into his grandmother's house. In a sense, he felt as though he were coming home. "It was such a tumultuous time going back and forth to South Carolina and all the trouble I had down there. I felt peace and calm back with my grandmother and knew I no longer had to put up with all the bullying and prejudices against me by the kids down there. It was just a whole different world, and it was very special to me because Grandma was there."

Once again, Eddie knew who and where he was. He could be proud of his Indian heritage and his dark skin. He knew he was safe with his grandmother, and no one would judge him because he was an Indian.

•••

When Eddie looks back on those years living with his grandmother in the little house on Ward Street, he thinks of her wonderful attitude toward life. "Grandma was born in 1890, and her name was entered on the Dawes Roll at the turn of the century. She was taller than most women and always had an air of a Cherokee princess about her. Sometimes she wore a colorful scarf on her head and always looked nice."

The Dawes Final Rolls were a federal census of those living in the Cherokee Nation and used to allot Cherokee land to individual citizens in preparation for Oklahoma statehood. Cherokee Nation citizenship only requires having one direct Cherokee ancestor listed on the rolls. Cherokee tribal members receive free healthcare, vocational training, college scholarships, housing assistance, and numerous other benefits.

Eddie's grandmother often talked to him about her childhood and how difficult her life was. "She was an orphan and was passed from one family to another. Some of the people where she lived were mean to her. She said all they wanted was someone, even a child, to work for them.

But she always had a gentle smile on her face when she told me how she was able to survive the harsh treatment at the hands of those who were supposed to take care of her."

There is emotion in his voice when he talks about his elderly, full-blood Cherokee Indian grandmother, who loved him and raised him from the fifth grade through high school and instilled in him many of the values he holds sacred today. "She was my rock and, more than anyone else, helped me make decisions that would determine my future destiny. She instilled confidence in me when she would say, 'You can do anything you want to do, be anything you want to be.' There's really no way to explain how she influenced my life. She once told me, 'You can stay here in Tahlequah and be a ditch digger or you can get an education and rise up and be a great success.' She made sure I was in school every day, and although I didn't have nice clothes like most of the other children, she always made sure my clothes were washed and ironed."

Her encouraging words were quite prophetic, for at that time she had no way of knowing that one day Eddie would become famous for his paintings and sculptures across America and in several foreign countries.

Today Eddie marvels at the great wisdom she shared with him. "She once told me, 'Eddie, if you think bitter thoughts, you're going to be bitter. Just remember, there's always a better day, if you look for it.' But perhaps the greatest lesson I ever learned from her was how to go through life with a good attitude and the importance of having a spiritual background—something to believe in."

Eddie learned another great lesson from his grandmother, a lesson about success. "She grew up in the Echota area near Stillwell, Oklahoma, and only finished the second grade in school. But she was remarkable and so very intelligent. She taught herself to read and write both English and the Cherokee language, and that's quite an accomplishment even for the Cherokee people. Writing the Cherokee language is very difficult."

Eddie proudly pointed out that she grew up with traditional Cherokee beliefs about the great Creator and about the close relationship between her people and nature but also was a faithful Presbyterian all her life.

Eddie and his grandmother were poor, lived in a small house, and, since they didn't have a car, walked nearly everywhere they went, even to school in the rain and snow. "Every school day I would walk down a hill that we called the 'Indian Trail' that crossed Town Branch and on to school."

Christmastime was always bittersweet for Eddie. He knew that his grandmother had barely enough money for them to get by and couldn't buy him a gift. "I remember at Christmastime people would come to our door and give us a basket of fruit. Grandma was always very gracious and received the basket—but I was embarrassed. . . . I knew they brought it to us because we were poor and probably wouldn't receive much of anything else for Christmas. You know, it's kinda sad when you are a kid and don't have any money and know you are not going to get any presents. But I tried not to be disappointed."[12]

One Christmas he received a great surprise. "I was about twelve years old and I said, 'Grandma, I really would like to have a basketball goal for Christmas.' I guess I was just dreaming, for I knew we were living on her meager old-age pension and we didn't have much money for anything other than food and clothing."

She was very compassionate toward him, saying, "That would be nice—maybe someday. I don't know how we could get one now. We just don't have the money."

However, Eddie was in for a big surprise. "On Christmas day, my uncle, Buzz Clay, who lived in the Welling community several miles east of Tahlequah, brought me a rough sapling off of a tree. I already had an old, worn-out basketball goal and he nailed some boards to that sapling, nailed the goal to the boards, then dug a hole and placed the sapling in the ground."

Eddie finally had a basketball goal. "I didn't have many friends of my own, except for Pete Vann, who was my age and lived a few houses down from us on Ward Street. But when I got the basketball goal, I made some new friends with the other kids in the neighborhood. I found an old, worn-out basketball, and we played and played and had a good time using that old goal until we wore it out."

There is a hint of nostalgia in his voice when he remembers those days. "That's one Christmas present I will never forget. Just an old basketball goal nailed to a small tree. It's quite different for kids today, who have all kinds of toys and things and Christmas presents every year."

Eddie and his grandmother often visited Buzz and his family out in the Welling community. While the older folks sat on the front porch talking about old times, he would go up into the hills and dream for hours about the future. "I can remember sitting on a hillside looking down at the crystal-clear waters of the Illinois River that sparkle in the morning sun and thinking, 'I never want to leave this place as long as I live—I love this place. It is so peaceful.'"

Although he enjoyed living with his grandmother Jane, and she loved him like a son, Eddie felt that his life was shrouded in mystery. He often remembers the time he met an elderly Cherokee woman wearing a colorful bandana. He was only four or five years old at the time and often wandered alone through the streets of Tahlequah. The woman told him something he would not understand until years later.

"She placed her hands on my shoulders, looked down at me, and said, 'You know, boy, I'm your grandmother, don't you?'"

"No ma'am, I don't know you."

"Yes, it's true."

"No, I already have a grandmother."

"Yes, I am your grandmother. One day you will know."

Then she walked away and Eddie never saw her again.

Meeting the old woman scared and confused him, for he didn't know what she was talking about. "I had a grandmother and didn't know anything about any other grandmother. Although I never met my mother's first husband, for he and my mother broke up when I was very young, I always thought he was my father, and no one ever told me different. However, from time to time, I would wonder about what the old woman told me on the streets of Tahlequah that day."

When he told his grandmother Jane what the woman said, as usual she chose her words with great wisdom. "Pay it no mind, Eddie. One day you'll know if you are supposed to know."

Years later, he learned that she was indeed his grandmother. "Her name was JoAnn Parris and her son Mose was my real father. I met him many years later at an art show in Arizona and tried to reach out to him, for I really wanted to get acquainted and learn as much as I could about my heritage. But I was really disappointed, for he didn't want anything to do with me."

As Eddie grew older, he faced a lot of temptations. "I ran around with some guys who smoked and drank, but out of respect for Grandma, I never took a drink, for I knew it would disappoint her. She was such a saintly woman and the pride of my life. I loved her with all my heart and I would never do anything to hurt her."

Eddie enjoyed going hunting with his brother Don, who was ten years older. "He and some of his friends would take me hunting in the woods southeast of Tahlequah on cold winter days. The woods were full of rabbits, and Don and his friends always shot a lot of them. Don always made me carry the rabbits back to town."

A broad grin creased Eddie's face when he remembered what Don did with the rabbits. "My brother and his friends would take the rabbits up on the hill to Lee Street, where all the black folks lived in Tahlequah, and trade them to this black guy for bootleg whiskey. Then they would drink and play cards all night. I was right there watching them."

But Don wouldn't let Eddie drink. "He always told me not to do those things."

They also would float down the Illinois River in an old flat-bottom boat and fish along the way. Eddie remembers they had a very unusual way of catching catfish. "Don would find an old telephone with a ringer that you would crank. It had a magneto on it and two electrical lines he would put into the water. I would crank the old phone and it would transmit an electrical current into the water. The shock wouldn't kill the fish, only stun them, and they would rise to the top. Then Don would get out of the boat and scoop up the fish."

Eddie was so young he had no idea that what they were doing was illegal in some states. "We weren't young outlaws, but kids do some crazy things. And we weren't doing it for sport; we cleaned and ate all the fish we caught."

Eddie was always proud of Don and looked up to him. "My brother went full circle. He dropped out of high school after his sophomore year and joined the army paratroops. After his discharge, he took the GED and entered Northeastern State University in Tahlequah. He lived with Grandma and me when he was going to Northeastern and was a good role model for me. He turned his life around and became a really good man. He made straight As and Bs and became a math teacher. He taught school in Albuquerque, New Mexico for twenty-five years."

One day Don gave Eddie some good advice. "You always have to be your own man and always do what's right."

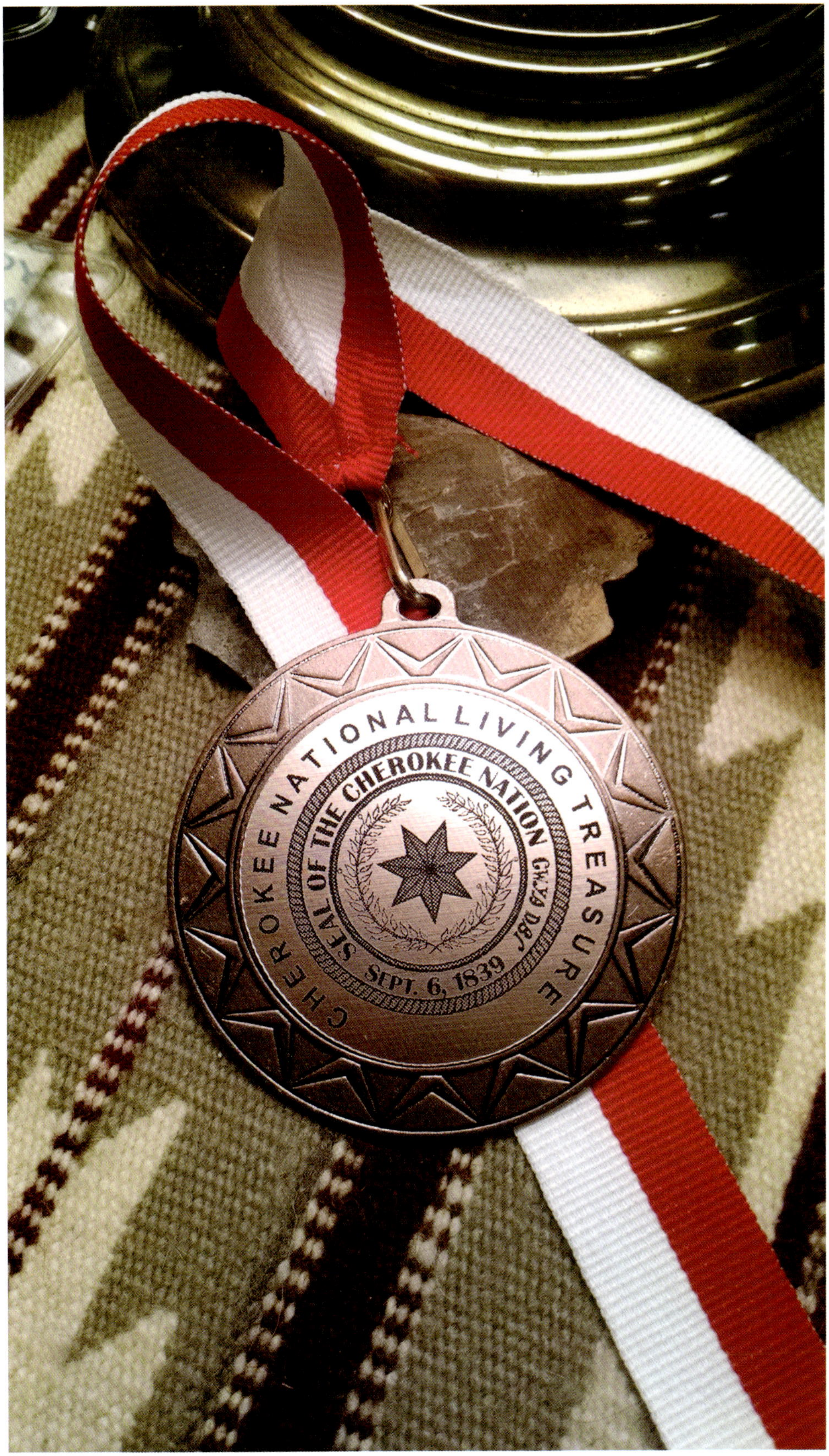

Cherokee National Treasure medallion

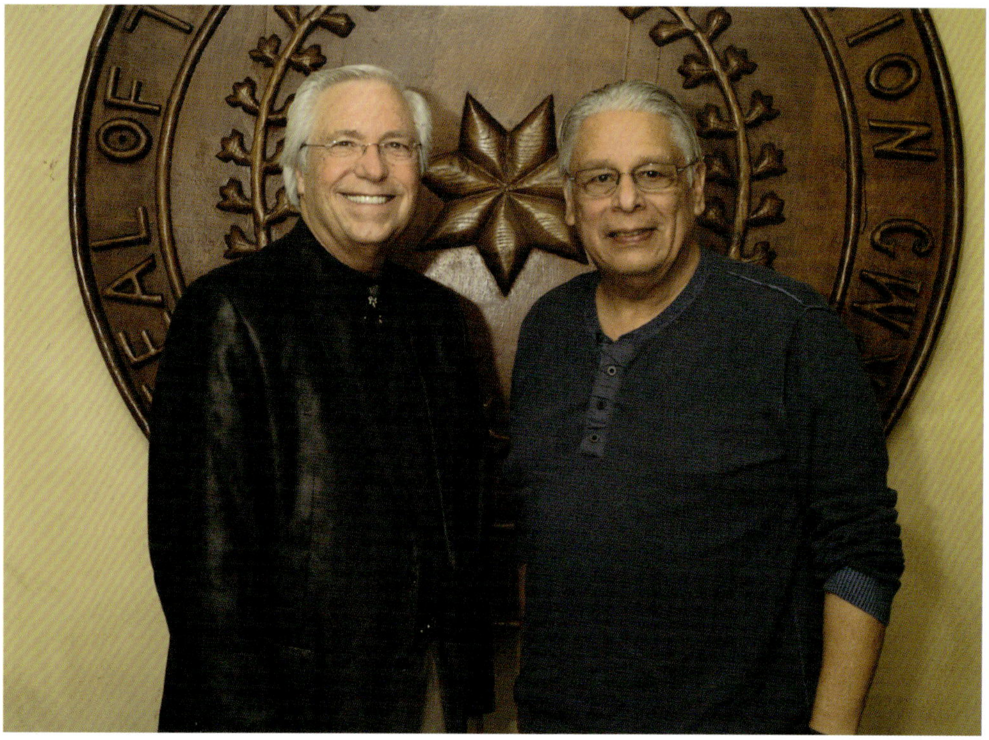

Eddie (right) with Chief Bill John Baker (Photograph by Brandon Scott)

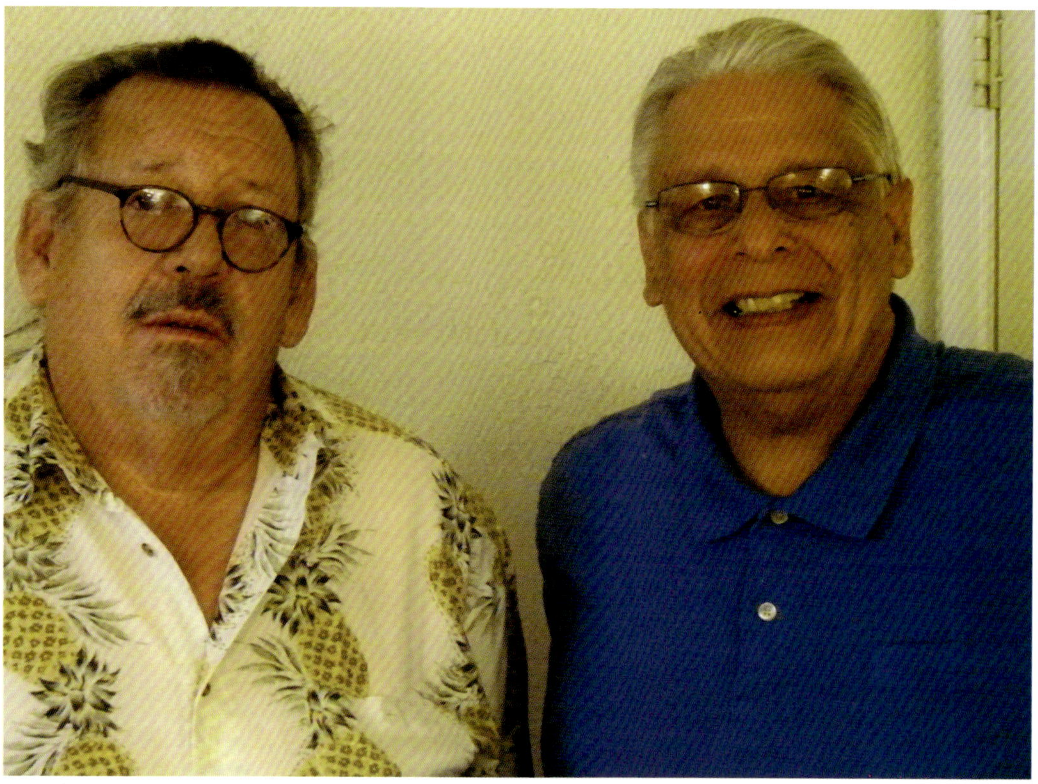

Eddie and his brother Jesse Hummingbird (left), also an acclaimed Native American artist

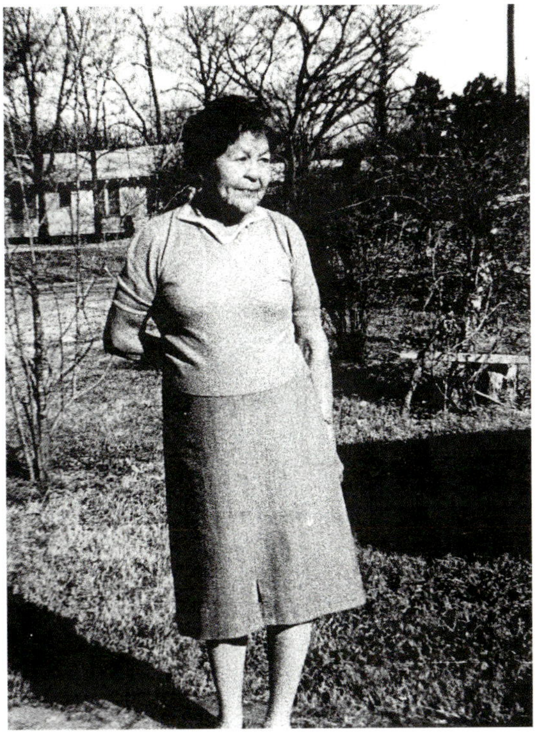

Eddie's grandmother Jane Batt Brackett

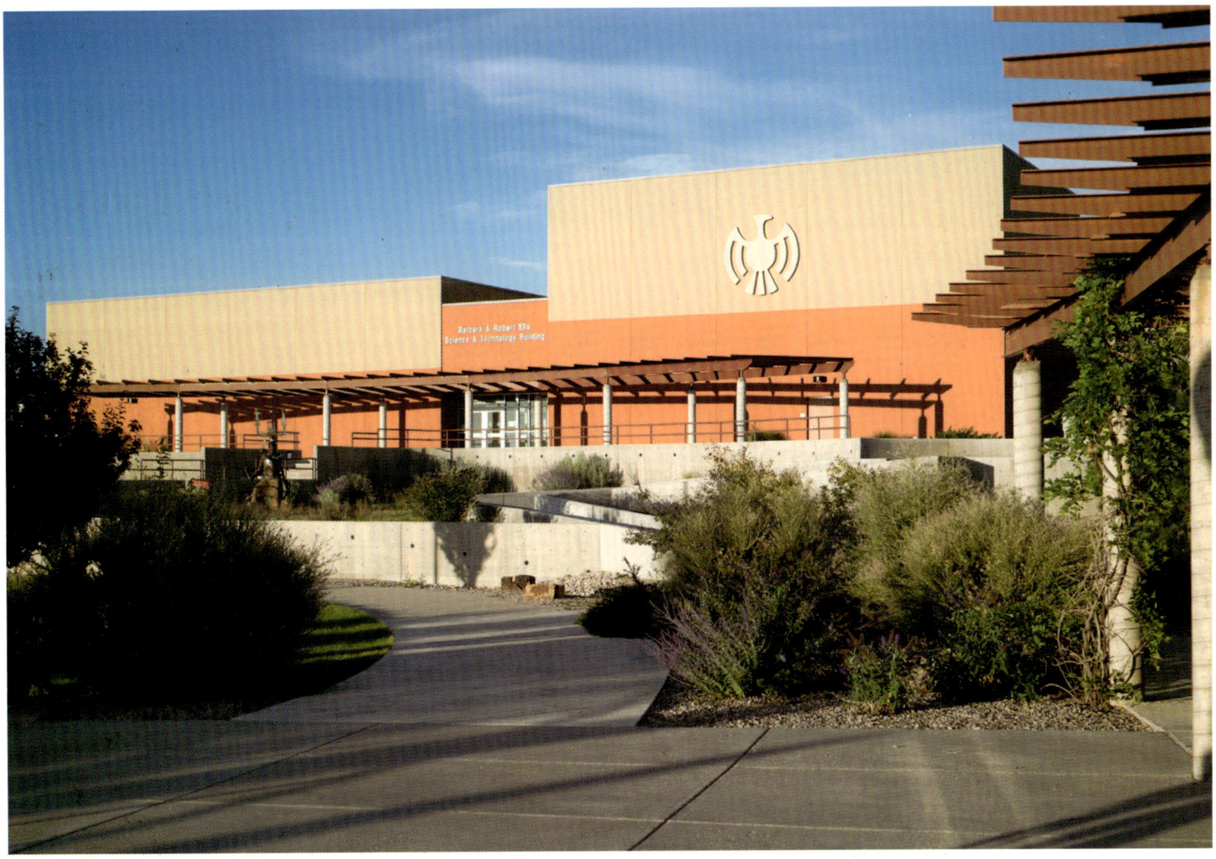

The Institute of American Indian Arts in Santa Fe, New Mexico, where Eddie graduated with honors

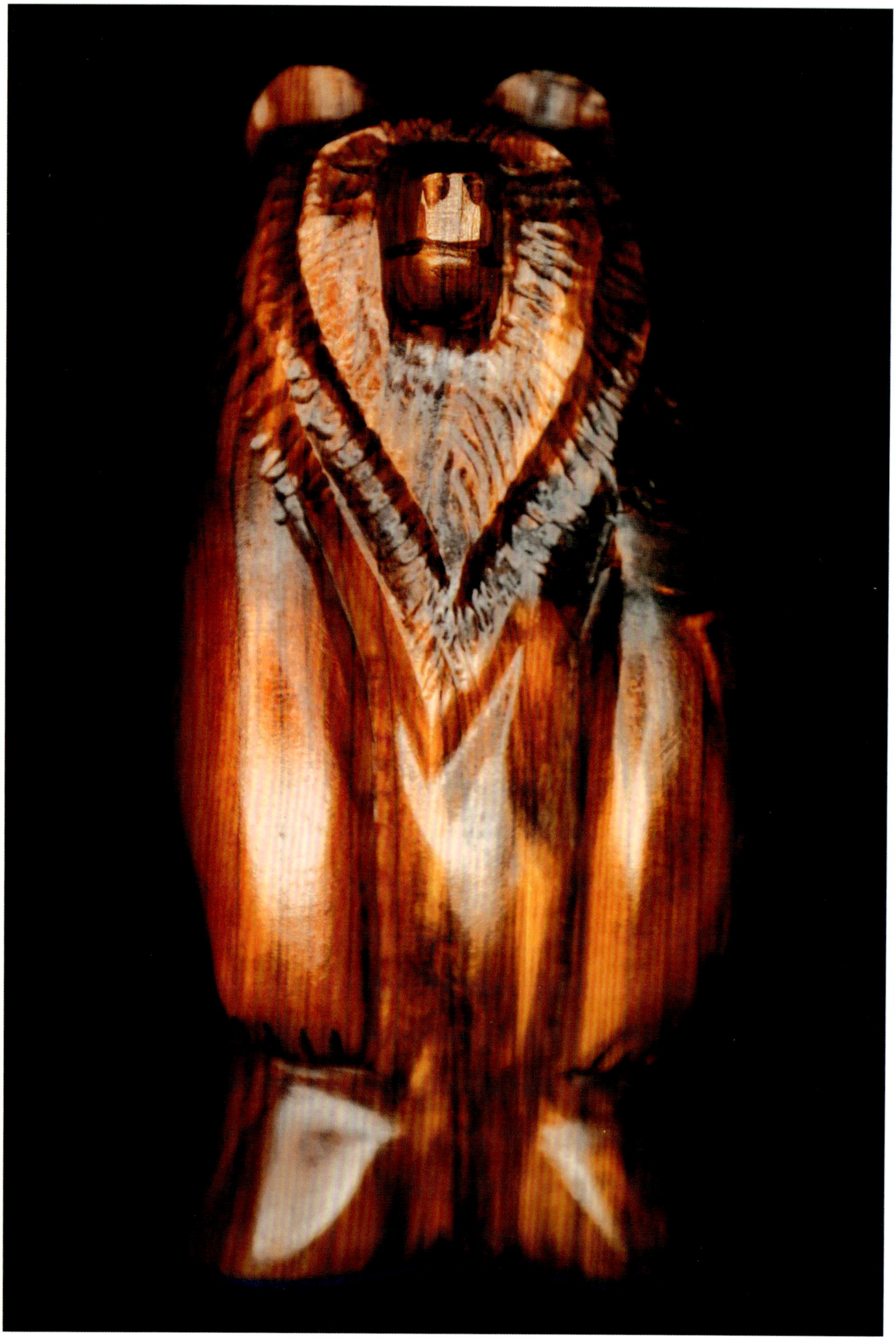

Bear carved from cedar

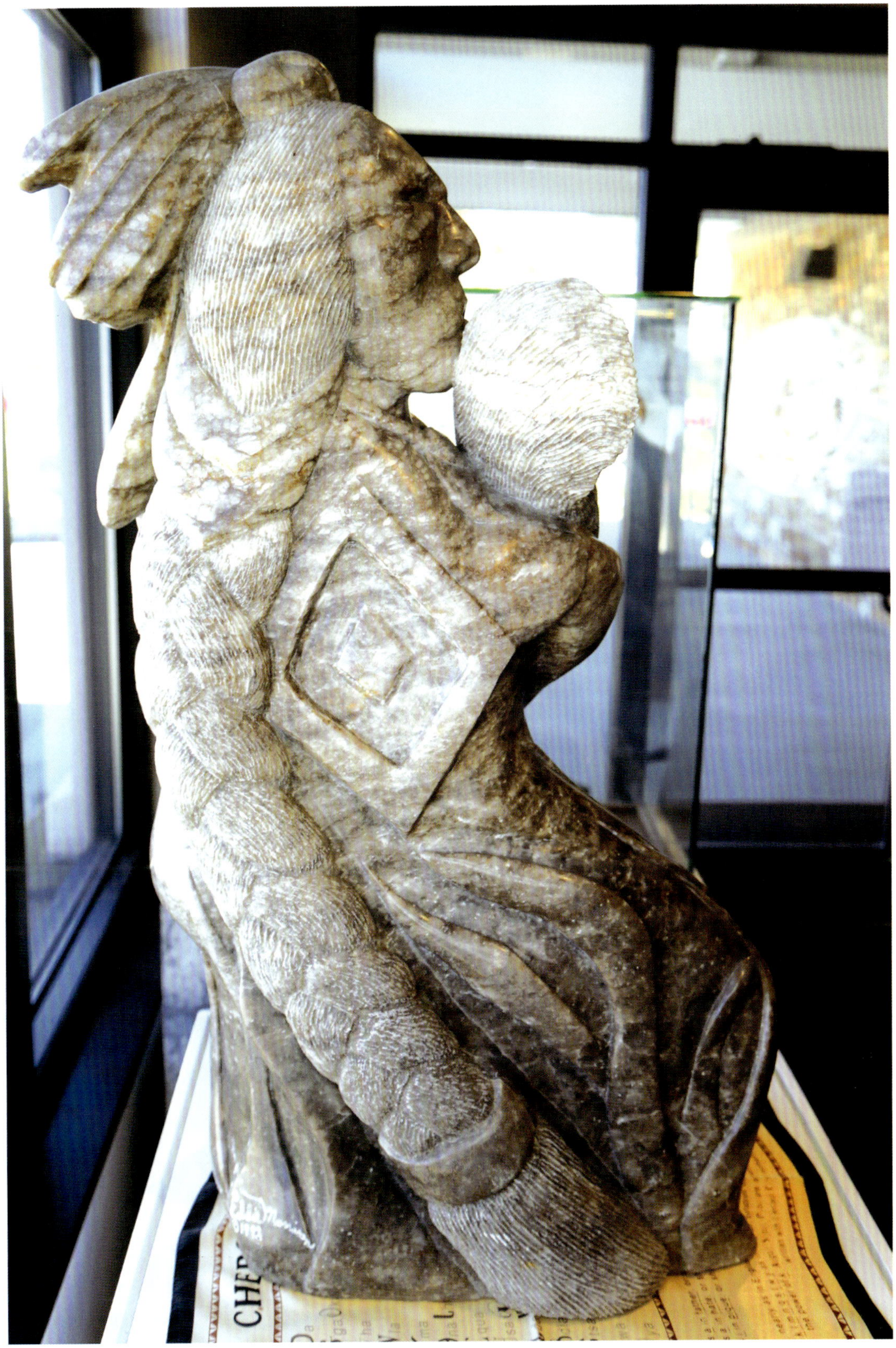

The Legend of the Ice Man and the Fire, *carved from alabaster and on display in the Cherokee Veterans Building*

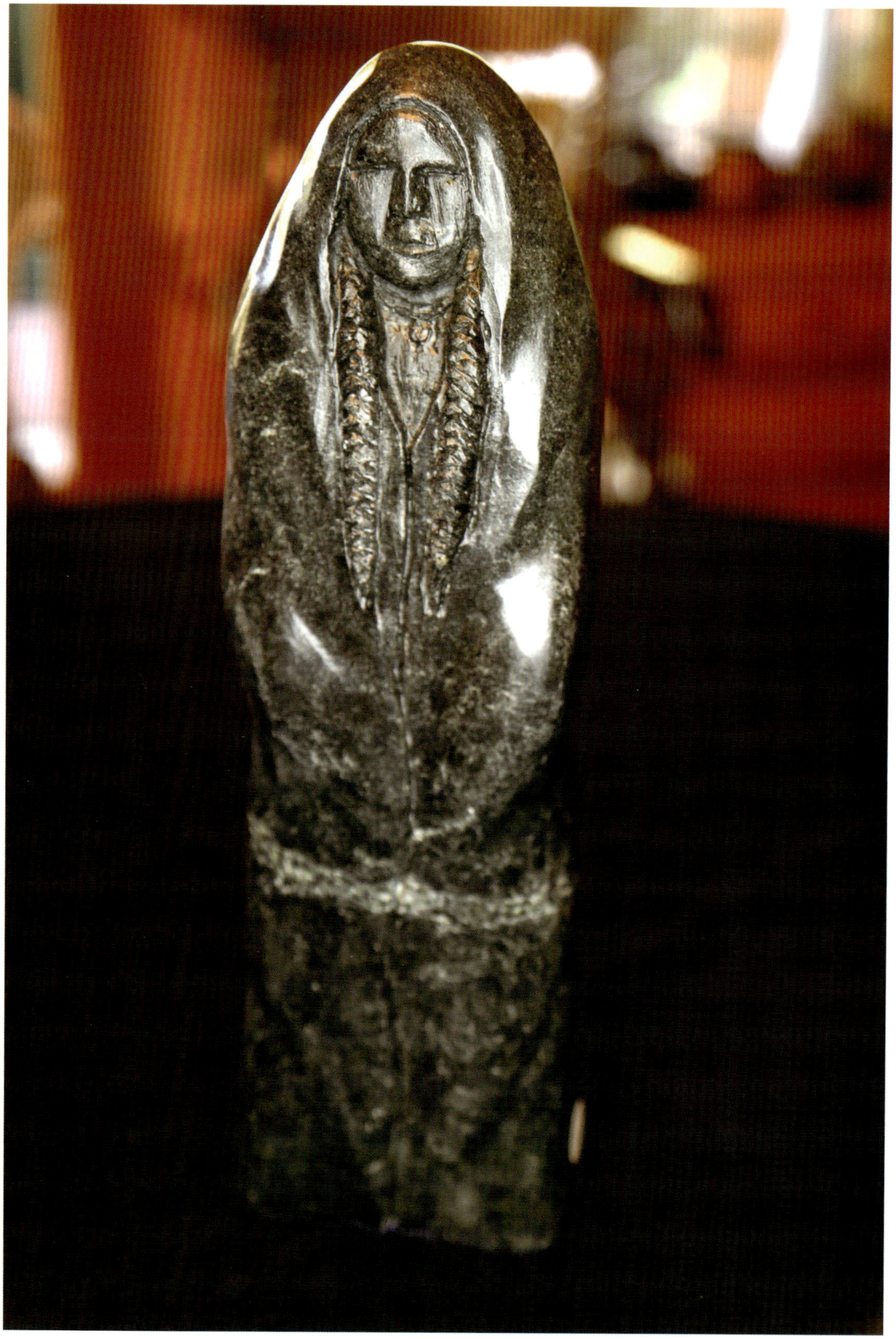

A noble Native American carved from steatite

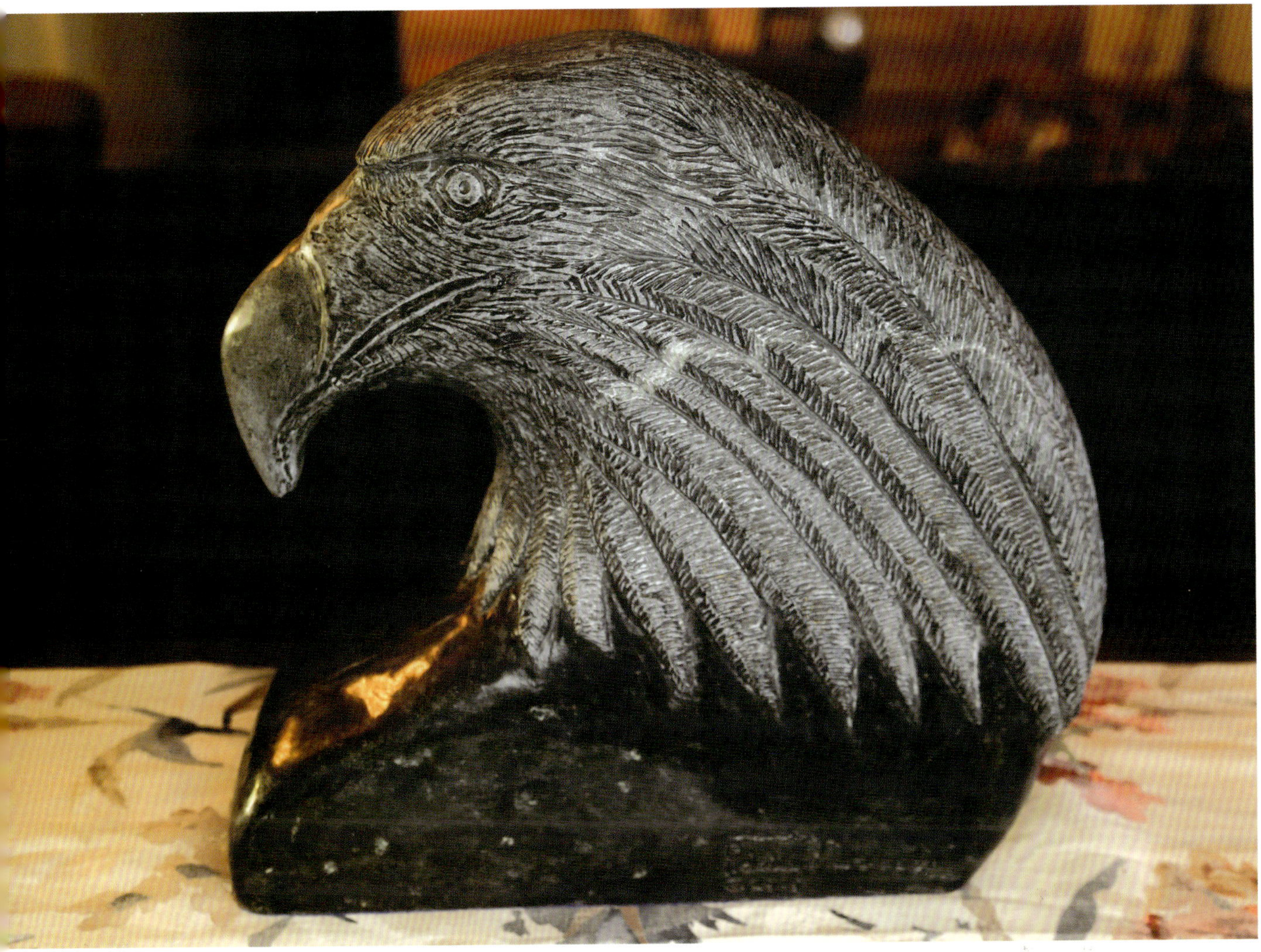

Eagle carved from Virginia steatite

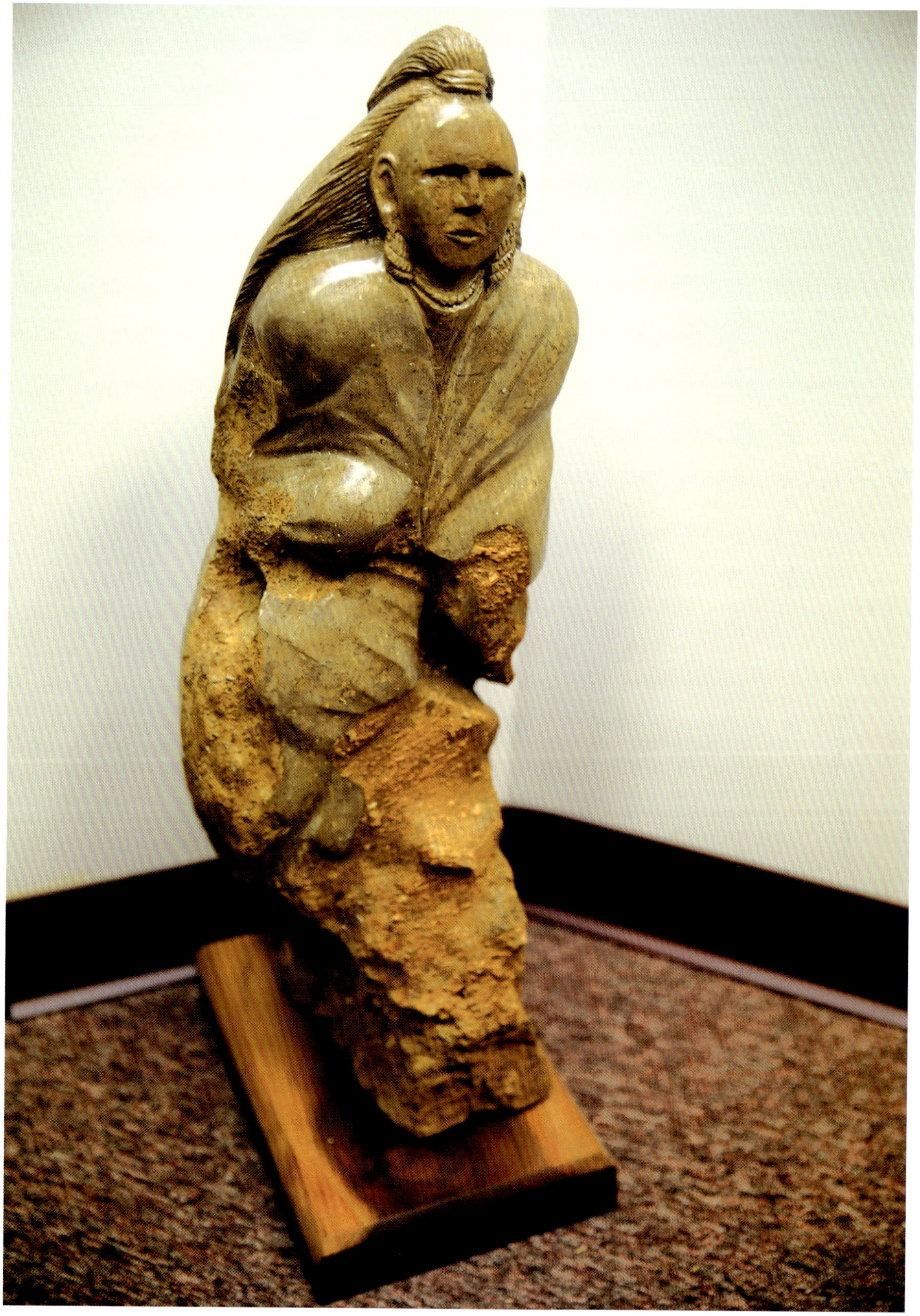

Cherokee Warrior, *carved from Oklahoma limestone* (Photograph by Brandon Scott)

Chapter Three

Transitions

Early one morning, Eddie was walking to Bagley Junior High School when he heard a motorcycle roaring down the street toward him. The rider stopped next to him and revved the engine.

"Where you going?" the rider asked.

"To school."

"Bagley?"

"Yes."

"Okay. I'm going to Bagley. Get on the back; I'll give you a ride."[1]

That was the day Eddie made his first friend at the school. "It was Jim Locke, who became my closest friend."

Jim also remembers that morning. "I was riding my motorcycle toward school when I noticed this guy walking down the street real slow with his head down. He looked to be about my age so I stopped and gave him a ride to school. When we rode up to the school all the other kids stood around in awe watching the two boys on a motorcycle. Eddie and I have had a great ride ever since."[2]

Something about Eddie always impressed Jim, and that was his attitude. "He had a great smile and good heart and you knew he was someone you wanted to be around."

Jim remembers they did all kinds of things together. "We would hang out together late at night, fishing on the Illinois River, and on weekends go camping or take canoe trips down the river, just the kinds of things small-town kids do."

According to Jim, he and Eddie were the original odd couple. "Eddie was always a quiet friend, never said too much, . . . always polite and deferential to others. On the other hand, I was outrageous, extroverted, and always looking to try something new."

Eddie had a built-in sense of morality that Jim admired. "He apparently learned that morality from his grandmother. He could never be talked into doing anything he didn't want to do or anything he thought was wrong. I never knew much about his family and never asked for it really didn't matter. I did see his grandmother a few times through the screen door at their house and knew that Eddie always had good things to say about her."

One cold November night, Jim, Eddie, and several of their friends went gig-fishing on the river. An icy wind blew, and Jim said that things didn't turn out exactly as they had planned. "There were about six of us in my car and we drove right down to the bank of the river, where we built a fire and found an old flat-bottom boat. We didn't know who it belonged to but decided to use it anyway.[3]

"We only had one gig, a sharp spear on a long pole. Two of us at a time would take the gig and a Coleman lantern so we could spot the fish in the water, and the others would stay by the fire on the bank. We never did see any fish but it was fun being on the river with Eddie and the other guys."

In the early-morning hours, they returned the boat, tied it to a tree, and prepared to go home. "The fire had pretty much died out so we all got in the car, but it wouldn't start. There we were on a cold, dark night on a dirt road near the river and it was freezing and we couldn't get the car started. So we built another fire, bundled up, and tried to stay warm. About daylight, a couple of men came along and gave us a jumpstart."

Jim said he lost track of Eddie after high school. "But a few years ago when I began attending high-school reunions in Tahlequah, we reconnected."

Jim noticed Eddie had changed. "He was the same old Eddie, mind you, but I sensed he was not so shy or quiet and had a newfound confidence I had never seen before. Today we communicate almost daily over the Internet, see each other as often as possible, and have dinner with mutual friends and relive a lot of happy memories."

Jim believes that Eddie deserves his great success. "He didn't have very much when he was young, like money or cars or anything like that. But he had something far more important—a bunch of kids who thought a lot of him and considered him their friend and still do. He has been my friend for many years, ever since that early morning he first jumped on the back of my motorcycle and we roared into the schoolyard together. I'm happy he calls me his friend."[4]

Dwain Denny is another one of Eddie's friends from Bagley and high school. "Eddie was a good student and really did well in all of his classes. He was very unusual; he could get along with everybody. I really liked being around him. We had a lot of fun together. Both of us liked to hunt and fish and float down the river on a raft. And we both liked the woods, where we hunted rabbits and squirrels. On weekends we would fish in the river or at Carter's Landing on Lake Tenkiller."[5]

Dwain had a car, an old 1951 Chevrolet. He and Eddie would get in that car and ride all around Tahlequah. It was old but that didn't matter. As long as it had a little gas in it, they were ready to go for a ride. Today Dwain and Eddie get together and talk over old times.

When Eddie entered Bagley, he began a wonderful adventure in education that would shape him into the man he is today. He enjoyed his junior-high and high-school years. "During that time, I started coming out of my shell and shed my mental hang-up of being afraid to carry on a conversation with people, as I tried to forget the bad experiences of the past."

After junior high, Eddie attended Tahlequah High School. When he was a sophomore he decided to go out for football, even though he weighed only 135 pounds and knew he was never going to have much of a football career. But he thought it might be fun. "Although I tried real hard, during the games I spent most of the time sitting on the bench watching the others play."

He enjoyed the out-of-town football games, even though he never got on the field. "On one trip, we all went into a restaurant and the waitress brought each of us a bowl with lettuce and tomatoes in it. I didn't know what it was. When I got home, I told Grandma about it and she said it was a salad. I had never seen a salad before and had never even heard of one."

After only a few weeks, Eddie tired of sitting on the bench, especially when the weather turned cold. He knew that all his friends in the bleachers were wrapped in blankets and keeping warm. "I also knew I was never going to play in the games, so I decided to quit. I turned in my uniform and walked away and didn't tell anyone."[6]

To his great surprise, quitting the team angered his coach, Benny Kiger. "Man, he really got steamed. Some of my friends told me he was mad and was looking for me. One day, I was getting ready to go to Isabel Baker's speech class on the third floor when the coach caught up with me and started reaming me out."

Coach Kiger could be very intimidating. Eddie had seen that often during the team workouts. "He was a big, tough guy and had been a star running back at Northeastern [State University, in Tahlequah]. Some believed he was good enough to play professional football. He started cussing me and called me every name in the book. He yelled, 'You're just a no-good quitter and you should have told me you were not going to play anymore!' He really pitched a fit."

Miss Baker came to the door to see who was yelling. "She jumped all over Coach Kiger. 'Benny, just stop right now. Get out of here and leave Eddie alone! It's time for his class.'"

Eddie smiled as he remembered the incident. "The coach looked like he had seen a ghost. He didn't know what to say to Miss Baker, so he turned and stomped away mad."

These many years later, he is still thankful Miss Baker rescued him that day. "He was so mad I thought he was going to hit me, but she put the fear of God in him. She had some courage and wouldn't put up with any foolishness from the coach or anyone else."

Years later, Miss Isabel Baker became Dr. Isabel Baker after she received her doctorate from Oklahoma State University. She taught there before teaching at Northeastern State University, her alma mater. Dr. Baker became one of the best-known educators in Oklahoma. She is the mother of Bill John Baker, the principal chief of the Cherokee Nation, and the state named her Mother of the Year in 1967. In 1991, Gov. David Walters appointed her to the Board of Regents of the Oklahoma State University System. She served for eight years, including one year as chairman. In 1993 she was named to the Oklahoma Women's Hall of Fame.

She still remembers having Eddie in her speech class. "In my forty-three years of teaching, I never had a student as special as Eddie Morrison. I had the opportunity to observe him and knew him well.

"Eddie was always on time for class and came to school with his clothes starched and ironed every day. He was quiet and soft-spoken but was popular with the teachers and his classmates. He always had a smile on his face and was a peacemaker when his friends got into it with one another."

She also remembered the incident with Coach Kiger outside her classroom. "The coach was out of line but I was pretty feisty myself in those days. Both Benny and I put the incident behind us and became friends and from time to time would have a good laugh when we remembered the encounter there in the school that day. He was really a good guy but lost his temper with Eddie. We worked together several years after that. But he never bothered Eddie again."[7]

Today Dr. Baker says she was always intrigued by Eddie's history. "He was raised by his elderly grandmother and much love was evident as they shared their lives together. I also followed Eddie's life and career after he graduated from high school. He went into the army for a time and later to Northeastern, where he excelled in the sciences. He received many honors as a medical technologist, but art seemed to always be calling him.

"He finally answered the call and went to art school and became a fulltime painter and sculptor. Today he and his art are respected and admired all over this land. He is truly a gentleman among men."[8]

As a junior in high school, Eddie joined the wrestling team. "Miss Baker's husband, Tim, was my coach. I really liked him, for he was a good coach and treated all of us with respect."

But just as Eddie didn't consider himself much of a football player, he also knew he was not a great wrestler. "I weighed only 135 pounds and had never wrestled before, so I didn't make the main team. My best friend, Jimmy Locke, and I were in the same weight division, and I couldn't beat him because he was a lot stronger than I was. So Coach Baker assigned me to the B-team. I won a few matches and had a lot of fun. In one match with a wrestler from Sequoyah Indian School, I pinned him real fast and Coach Baker, announcing the winner, said, 'That's our own Tiger Morrison.' Everyone laughed and clapped their hands."

Eddie always remembered what coach Baker said that day and always liked the sound of "Tiger Morrison."

•••

Although Eddie was not a champion football player or wrestler, he was a good bow hunter and really enjoyed going to the woods and being around the beauty of nature. "My friend Pete Vann's father, Lyman, was a world-champion cornstalk shooter. Pete's father crafted the bows and arrows in his home on Ward Street not far from Grandma's house. Pete and I learned to shoot them. Then my brother Don taught me to deer hunt with the bow and arrows. I shot my first deer when I was about seventeen."[9]

Cornstalk shooting dates back to Cherokee hunter and warrior competitions using their bows and arrows. Their target would be a large bundle of cornstalks, so that their arrow tips would not break. The sport remains popular among Cherokees today. The cornstalk bundles are three feet long and stacked one foot deep and three feet high. They are bound by hickory sticks driven into the ground and tied together at the top. Only a handmade bow of a wood such as bois d'arc, hickory, and black walnut may be used. Each shooter shoots two arrows, and the shooter whose arrow has the deepest penetration into the bundle of stalks is the winner.

Eddie said Lyman made the bows and arrows from raw wood. "We'd sit and watch him for hours, carving a bow out of the wood, and it just fascinated me that he could make something out of nothing. That's the way I feel today. To see something come from nothing and go into something is exciting to me."[10]

Today Eddie says it was a great privilege to live on the same street with the famous cornstalk shooter. "I was always fascinated as I watched him make several bows from selected bois d'arc wood. He would shave them and shape them for hours, turning the wood into a beautiful bow. And he would also do the tedious tasks of arrow making, as a cornstalk arrow requires a special point that must penetrate the cornstalks, which is how the shooter scores his points. Sometimes he would go with me to visit my uncle Buzz out at Welling and he would go to the woods and look for bois d'arc trees, cut off a few limbs, and take them home to his workshop, where he could lay them out to dry and cure."

Lyman Vann's ingenuity in working with the bows and arrows always amazed Eddie. "He would take an old spoon and pound it and shape it with a file, until it was sharp pointed and would fit the arrow shaft. The shaft was shaved and shaped much in the same manner as the wooden bow, which propels the heavy arrow the long distance required in the cornstalk shoot." Lyman used dogwood limbs for his arrows. "Grandma had some dogwood trees in her backyard, and he would come over and cut some straight limbs off the trees and make arrows out of them."

Watching Lyman Vann and the other old-time Cherokee Indians with their homemade bows and arrows at the cornstalk shoot always fascinated Eddie. "The shooters were always very accurate with their shots." One year Lyman won the bow shoot during the Cherokee National Holiday. Eddie was proud of him.

Eddie greatly respected Lyman. "He worked at the Sequoyah Indian School about five miles south of Tahlequah. Since he didn't have a car, he walked the five miles to work each morning and five miles home each evening."

When Eddie learned that Lyman Vann had passed away, he knew that an important part of Cherokee culture passed away with him and he would be greatly missed. "He had a real influence on my life, and I carry many happy memories of his life and work. After he passed away, Pete followed in his father's footsteps and now carries on the bow and arrow tradition in the family."

Several years ago, Pete did something very special for Eddie. "He made a bow for me and gave me two arrows from that same dogwood tree in Grandma's backyard. That really meant a lot to me, and I treasure the gift."

Eddie said there is a real excitement in taking just a raw piece of stone or wood and turning it into something beautiful. "It gives you a real good feeling to see that, too. That's part of the enjoyment and love of being a sculptor, I guess."[11]

Although he was well liked in school, Eddie didn't have a lot of close friends. And since he was poor and didn't have a car, he didn't have much opportunity to date. "But it really didn't matter that much. Some of the girls' parents wouldn't let them go out with me because I was Indian. I'm really glad that today those barriers have been broken down here in Tahlequah and it doesn't seem to matter that much."

Faye Hammons was different and the only real girlfriend Eddie had all through high school. She remembered very well when she and Eddie were special friends. "He didn't have a car, so we were limited where we could go and what we could do. He was just a poor Indian boy but we were friends and I always enjoyed being with him."[12]

After high school, they went their separate ways—he to become a nationally acclaimed artist and she to a successful cosmetology business. They would meet forty years later and renew their friendship.

Eddie graduated from high school in the spring of 1964. "It was a glorious occasion, not only for me, but also for Grandma. She wore a big smile on her wrinkled, wizened face and tears of pride in her dark brown eyes. She hugged me and said, 'I'm proud of you, but you're not through yet, Eddie. You're going to college.'"

That day, Eddie knew he and his grandmother had weathered the storms of life. "We came out of near poverty, living in a small home in a poor neighborhood, not even having all of the bare necessities of life, but we made it, Grandma and me. I will always look back on those days with great pride in my heart."

After high school, Eddie met a young woman by the name of Gail Stepp, and after a courtship, they married and had one son, Ron, and a daughter, Monica. Although the marriage did not last, they remain friends. Ron has had a very successful career as a forestry firefighter with the federal government's Bureau of Land Management. Monica lives in Broken Arrow, Oklahoma, and works in transportation.

All through high school, Eddie had a dream. "I wanted to join the United States Marine Corps. I wanted be a marine, wear the nice uniform, and serve my country. So I went to the Marine Corps recruiting office and told the recruiter I wanted to enlist for three years. He was pleased and the first thing he did was give me a test, which I passed with flying colors."

But Eddie had a problem—a big one. "I was only seventeen years old and I had to be eighteen to join the Marines or else my grandma, my legal guardian, would have to sign a document which would give me permission."[13]

Things fell apart for Eddie and his dream. "The recruiter came to our house to talk to Grandma. He told her he thought I was going to be a fine marine and said, 'I hope you will let him join up for three years.'"

His grandmother wasn't the least bit interested in talking to the recruiter, although he was a very nice young man. Eddie sat still and wondered what she was going to say. "She looked the recruiter square in the eyes and, without hesitation, said, 'No!' And she meant it—just put her foot down."

Then she turned to Eddie. "You're not going to the Marines for three years, for you will be gone from home too long and you need to go to school."

The young recruiter thanked her, shook hands with Eddie, and left.

That ended Eddie's dream of being a marine. "I was so disappointed. My older brother Don had been in the paratroopers. I was so proud of him and how he jumped out of airplanes and landed safely on the ground. I thought that would be really exciting. I had some uncles who had served in World War II and the Korean War. I had seen pictures of them and they looked so fine in their army uniforms. But it looked like I would have to wait a year until I was eighteen to join anything because Grandma just wouldn't change her mind."

Then Eddie came up with another idea and decided to share it with her, hoping she would be a little more understanding this time. "I checked out the Army Reserves and learned I could go to basic training for only six months and then come back home and go to summer camp for training a couple of times a year."

He knew it all depended on his grandmother. "So I went to her and told her about the Army Reserves, that I would only be gone for six months. And she said, 'Okay, I'll sign the papers since you'll only be gone for six months.'"[14]

A new adventure began in his life, as Eddie and seven or eight of his friends joined the Army Reserves.

The army sent the young recruits to Fort Polk, in the piney eoods of west-central Louisiana, for six months of basic training. Eddie soon caught on that this would be no picnic. He decided that the giant military base must be the hottest, bleakest, and most snake-and mosquito-infested place on earth.

He and the other raw recruits also faced a rude awakening regarding army discipline. "It was a new and different world. The drill sergeants were right when they called that first week 'Hell Week.' The very first day, they yelled and screamed at us so much I was ready to go home to Grandma, where it was safe and quiet."

Eddie didn't like any of the drill instructors and thought they were way too rough on the new recruits—especially him. "They were hardened World War II and Korean War veterans and were really tough. Sometimes they would slap us and hit us with their fists. Since I only weighed 135 pounds, I kept my mouth shut and tried not to make them mad."

However, one of the sergeants turned out to be a kind but firm drill instructor, and one day he gave Eddie some good advice. "He told me if I could make it through basic training, it would make a man out of me and I would be able to handle most anything life would throw at me. I sensed in my heart that he was right so I decided to stick it out, and I did."

After the encouraging word from the sergeant, he did his best to excel on the rifle range, obstacle courses, intense physical training, and two-mile run carrying full field gear. "I managed to pass all the tests, but I was glad when the six months ended. I sure wanted to get back to Tahlequah."

During his time at Fort Polk, he noticed that some of the units received orders to ship out to fight the communists in Vietnam. "Our unit was never called up, and I've always wondered about the guys who went halfway around the world to fight a war. I'm sure many of them died over there. Most of them were all just boys right out of high school."

After basic training, Eddie returned to Tahlequah to live with his grandmother. She was glad to see him, and he was glad to be home.

As he looked back, Eddie wasn't exactly sure what to say about his days in the army. "It was quite a trip, but serving my country was a great privilege." He knew he learned a lot of discipline and understanding that would serve him well on his journey through life.

The Army Reserves still had plans for him. They assigned him to a quartermaster unit in Muskogee, Oklahoma, where he reported for active duty one weekend each month. "And every summer I also went to summer camp for two weeks of additional training at either Fort Hood in Killeen, Texas, or Fort Sill in southern Oklahoma." Eddie remained in the reserves for another six years.

In 2010, the Cherokee Nation Tribal Council honored Eddie for his army service. "This honor means a great deal to me. While serving in the military, I was always proud to be an American and proud to share the legacy of my Cherokee ancestors with others."

The Nation also has purchased one of Eddie's stone carvings to place in the new Cherokee Veterans Building. It is titled *The Legend of the Ice Man and the Fire*. Eddie said it is a large piece carved from New Mexico alabaster. "I am really honored to have one of my sculptures in the Veterans Building, since I, too, am a veteran and I have a great respect for all the men and women who have served our country."[15]

One day after Eddie returned from Fort Polk, he and some friends went rabbit hunting in a heavily wooded area several miles southeast of Tahlequah. "That day it was freezing cold. The brush was real thick, and I was watching for a rabbit to come out of a thicket when I felt something hit my legs. It knocked my feet out from under me. One of my friends had accidentally shot me with his twelve-gauge shotgun. The pellets hit both of my legs, my ankles and feet. I recovered but some of those pellets are still in my legs. I guess it could have been a lot worse. My friend really felt bad for shooting me."

Eddie's grandmother continued to remind him that if he wanted to succeed in life, he needed a good education. After his tour of duty with the army, he knew that college would be a welcome change. So in September 1965, he enrolled at Northeastern.

On May 7, 1851, the Cherokee Nation founded the Cherokee National Female Seminary in Tahlequah. It would become the Northeastern State Normal School, Northeastern State Teachers' College, and then Northeastern State University. Northeastern (NSU) is Oklahoma's fourth-largest university and one of the oldest institutions of higher learning west of the Mississippi River. Today, about 25 percent of the students self-identify as American Indian. Many courses focus on Native American linguistics, and Cherokee-language education is offered as a major.

The Cherokee Nation provided scholarships for Indian students, but Eddie worked part-time jobs for additional income. "I worked for Luther Hammons at the Hammons Electrical Company in Tahlequah for one dollar an hour and later drove a milk truck to and from Springdale, Arkansas, to bring milk back to the people of Tahlequah. The extra money helped my grandmother and me make ends meet."

At first, Eddie was somewhat ambivalent as to what he should study. He thought initially that he wanted to be a doctor. "But I was aware of my limitations. I took several premed courses but later decided medicine was not the life for me."

Eddie majored in biology and chemistry. "But when I graduated, I wondered what in the world I was going to do with those degrees and where I was going to find a job."

Not knowing exactly what he wanted to do, Eddie applied for a position with an oil service company in Houston, Texas, and was hired as a salesman. "I still had a problem talking to people. However, I must have done something right, for they promoted me and trained me to become a sales service engineer. I became the company's branch-office manager in Odessa in West Texas. But I never ever enjoyed the job."[16]

Eddie was restless. He didn't like West Texas and wished he was back in Tahlequah. "I knew there must be some job I would enjoy more than being a sales service engineer for an oil company. It just seemed like a dead end to me."

One day while reading a trade magazine, he saw an article about a program for medical technologists at St. John's Hospital in Tulsa. "Since I had degrees in biology and chemistry, I thought perhaps I would qualify for the job."

Although he was somewhat apprehensive, he filled out an application and was accepted into the St. John's Medical Technology School. "I spent a year there, and when I graduated, I went to work for the hospital as a medical technologist. It was a very important job. We analyzed blood specimens. The doctors relied on our reports completely for their diagnoses and treatments."

While working at St. John's, he met Dr. Bryce Bliss, the chief pathologist. He was a graduate of the old Central High School in Tahlequah and Northeastern before medical school. "I knew Bryce was from one of the most prominent families in Tahlequah. When he found out I was from Tahlequah, he promoted me to evening shift supervisor, where I remained for four years."

It was 1976, and things were going very well for Eddie. He had a good job and enjoyed his work. The medical staff at St. John's respected him.

That year he met and married Vicki Nulik, who was from Caldwell, Kansas. The marriage produced a delightful daughter, Jennifer.

Chapter Four

New Beginnings

Things seemed to be looking up for Eddie. He had a family with a daughter on the way and a good job. But for some reason, the restlessness hidden deep in his soul would not go away. He struggled with it day and night.

Although he was very successful at St. John's, for some time he had felt in his heart that something more was waiting for him just around the corner. "I enjoyed being a medical technologist, and the people at St. John's treated me with great respect. But I had the feeling deep down in my heart that I would soon enter a new season in my life, a new beginning."

There was an air of mystery in the way he felt. "I began to think about art, and the more I thought about it, the more I was convinced that I had to find the key that would open the door for my dream—and the pathway that would lead me into a bright, new, and mysterious world that I knew virtually nothing about."

Eddie desired to reach out and create something, do something more than he had ever done before, and the desire would not go away. He knew that it had something to do with art. "But what?" he wondered. "I'm no artist."

To satisfy the yearning, he bought some art supplies—including paint and canvases—and started drawing with pen and ink. "My first drawing was of *Cherokee Pow Wow Eagle Dancers,* and I thought it looked pretty good. I did several others. I found that I really enjoyed drawing and painting and received a lot of satisfaction when I looked at what I had done."[1]

Although Eddie worked long hours in the lab at St. John's, he couldn't wait to get home at night to paint and create more pen-and-ink drawings. Soon he realized that his heart was in his art. But at that time, he had no idea where it would lead him.

While browsing through the local newspaper one day, Eddie noticed an article about a planned exhibit at the Philbrook Museum of Art in

Tulsa. In the article, the curator of the museum invited artists to submit their works to be considered for the show.

Eddie checked the date on the newspaper to make sure it was current and read the article again. Suddenly he felt that this was something he had been waiting and hoping for, a chance to show someone—anyone—his work.

That afternoon, he looked over all of his pen-and-ink drawings and tried to decide which ones to take to the museum. "The one I liked best was my *Indian Pow Wow Dancers*. But I had other pen-and-inks of an *Indian Stick Ball Player* and a young Cherokee boy shooting a squirrel with a blowgun."

While living in Tulsa, Eddie and his wife, Vicki, had visited the museum on several occasions, and he knew that it housed famous art collections from around the world. He felt a little nervous as he walked up the steps, opened the front door, and stepped into the office area. "Although the pictures weren't even framed, I asked a lady at a desk where I should go to submit my drawings for the show, and she directed me to the office of the curator of the museum."

Several days later, when he had not heard back from the museum, he wondered if his desire to become an artist was sheer fantasy. Then he received a letter. "I saw the Philbrook name and logo on the envelope and was so excited I could hardly get it open. When I finally opened it, I wanted to shout, because the letter was a notice from the director of the show that they had accepted my drawings. I knew a lot of people would be visiting the show and see my drawings."[2]

Later, when the exhibit opened, Eddie walked into the museum and saw his drawings right beside the works of famous artists from all across America. "Standing there in the museum that day, I thought that perhaps I did have a future in art. I hoped that some other doors would open for me and my work."

The Philbrook event marked the beginning of his new career. The show gave him a lot of good exposure, as many people, including representatives from various galleries in Oklahoma and other states, saw his work and apparently were impressed. He began receiving letters from all over the country inviting him to join other exhibits.

Today, Eddie is well aware that the museum's acceptance of his first drawings was just a small beginning. "But it was a beginning, and for that I was thankful."

Sad news dampened Eddie's elation over his success with his drawings. In December of 1976—three days before Christmas—he received a phone call from his uncle Chuck Brackett in Tahlequah, about Chuck's mother. "Grandma Jane is dead."

Eddie tried to speak, but the words stuck in his throat.

"She passed away peacefully last night. She was eighty-six, you know."

Eddie regained his composure and wiped away the tears. "Thank you, Chuck, I'll miss her. We'll all miss her. We'll leave for Tahlequah in the morning."

Eddie remembers a mystical experience he had the night his grandmother died, an experience he has never fully understood. "The night she passed away, I don't know if I was dreaming, but right before Chuck called I felt like she was standing right beside my bed. It's one of those things I just can't explain, but I know what I felt.

"I know God works in mysterious ways, and I guess there are some things we're not supposed to understand. We call it faith."

When Eddie and his family arrived in Tahlequah, he went to the funeral parlor at the Reed-Culver Funeral Home to pay his last respects to the grandmother who raised him and whom he dearly loved. As he stood by the casket and looked down at her saintly remains, all the years of trials and the struggle for survival flashed through his mind. He remembered her stately demeanor, the colorful scarves, the encouraging words, and her desire for her beloved Eddie to do something great with his life. He recalled her faith in God, her love for her church, and, even in the worst of times, her abiding belief that there were better days ahead for him if he would do his best and never quit.[3]

He vowed that day to forever be faithful to her vision. "I will always live my life in the shadow of her love. For one thing was certain, something I never doubted—she loved me."

When they laid her to rest in the Tahlequah Cemetery, Eddie knew that a woman who showed her greatness in small ways had passed into the future for her reward, a reward for how she lived her life and the lives she touched. And he knew that heaven was a better place because she was there. Eddie performed one last act of love for her that day, as he served as one of the pallbearers.

About that time, another major change impacted Eddie and his family. Vicki's relatives lived in Caldwell, Kansas, and she wanted to be near them.

Their daughter, Jennifer, loved being around her grandparents. Eddie thought it would be a good idea to leave the big city and settle down in the small farming community located in the south-central part of the state.

Caldwell—known as the "Border Queen"—was famous for the Old Chisholm Trail that in an earlier generation passed through the town. Founded in 1871, it was one of six famous "cow towns" in the state, once known for cowboys, saloons, gambling, and violence. Eddie had visited there several times. It was also known for the Cherokee Strip and the Ghost Rider silhouettes that could be seen on a bluff east of the city.

When Pres. Andrew Jackson forced the Cherokees out of their homes and lands in Georgia and other eastern states, the government gave them vast areas of land in what is now Oklahoma. Then the government took two million acres away from the Cherokees and opened it up to homesteaders. The Cherokee Strip was the area in Kansas where the homesteaders lined up to make the run for the land.

Eddie resigned his job at St. John's, thanked Dr. Bliss for his confidence in him and for promoting him, and moved his family to Kansas. "Since no one was living in Vicki's grandmother's place out in the country, we decided to live there for awhile. It was an old home, but the country was a good place for Jennifer to grow up and it was a wonderful change for me, for I enjoyed living away from the big city."[4]

A few weeks after they moved to Caldwell, Eddie received a letter from Kansas City informing him of a Native American Art Show in the Kansas City Plaza and inviting him to display his work. "When I read the letter, my mind began spinning at warp speed, for I didn't have a clue about what it was like to display my work in a major art show or anywhere else. But by that time I had done some acrylic paintings. So I took them, along with several of my pen-and-inks, and drove toward Kansas City.

"All along the route, I kept wondering if I was doing the right thing. It was still new to me, and I knew the road to success as an artist would be long and winding and would require major changes in my life and that of my family. I hoped I was up to it."

When he arrived, the show organizers had a table ready for him to display his art. "I couldn't believe it. There I was sitting at a table with famous Indian artists all around me and people coming and going and looking at and buying my art. I'll always remember Kansas City—that's where it all started. It was a good feeling getting paid for my work."

Eddie made a life-changing decision that night in Kansas City. "This is what I want to do for the rest of my life."

Although he was experiencing some success selling his works of art, he knew he needed additional income to support his family. He learned that the J. B. Hunt Trucking Company was looking for drivers, and he knew that the pay would be good. "So for a brief period I drove that big eighteen-wheeler all over the United States. It was quite a trip."

Eddie knew he was doing the right thing driving the truck to support his family, but art continued to be a consuming passion in his life. He dreamed of being a successful artist and took his knives and wood with him on the long trips. When he would pull over for the night, he would carve objects while resting. "One night a fierce snowstorm stopped all traffic on the highway, and I had several days to work on my art."

Then a serious accident caused him to rethink being a trucker. "I was driving that big International cab-over semi, pulling 40,000 pounds through Paris, Texas, when a car ran a stop sign and pulled right out in front of me. I hit him broadside and totaled his car."[5]

The wreck pinned Eddie in the cab of his truck, and while he tried to free himself and get out, he could hear a woman in the other car screaming. "I was afraid the truck might burst into flames, so I tried frantically to get loose and finally got out. But that accident scared me to death and I decided to give up being a trucker."

By chance, he learned there was an opening for a medical technologist at the St. Francis Hospital in Wichita, Kansas, about sixty miles from Caldwell. "I applied for the job and they hired me. I was glad I had my training, for I could work at the hospital during the day and with my art during the evenings."

One day he saw an advertisement in *Southwest Art Magazine* for a stone-carving class in Marble, Colorado. It would be taught by the renowned Native American sculptor Allan Houser.

"I had read a lot about Allan Houser and knew this Chiricahua Apache artist was well known as the Father of Native American sculpture. So I saved up the $400 tuition for the class, drove to Colorado, and took the course."

A big surprise awaited him when he arrived in Marble. "I felt out of place when I looked around and saw I was the only Indian in the class. But what an honor it was to be there learning from the most famous Indian sculptor in the world, the man people called the 'Michelangelo of the West.'"

Houser took a special interest in Eddie, perhaps because they were both Indians. Houser asked him all kinds of questions about his background and why he wanted to work with stone. He took Eddie under his wing, and Eddie considered that a great opportunity to learn and a great honor to be studying under such a gifted craftsman.

During the stone-carving class at Marble, Eddie had a keen sense that he should listen to everything Houser said. "He was a great man and a great artist, but he also had a big heart and a desire to help others. I've tried to emulate him, for there was no pretense in him; he was no prima donna. When I talked to him, he would listen to me as though I was important to him. It made me think, 'This is the kind of man I want to be.'"

Those were great days of learning for Eddie. "Houser told me the best way to learn was to watch him, every move he made. From that time forward, I watched him like a hawk and even took pictures of him as he worked."

Houser also told him that it's good to look at other artists' works and learn from them. "But as soon as you can, find your own way, your own style."

Eddie believes he has done that.

During one class assignment, the students were instructed to begin work on a sculpture under Houser's supervision. "As we worked, he would give us pointers on the stone we were carving—an idea here, a suggestion there. He helped us bring our carvings to life."

One day, Houser stepped over to where Eddie was working on a large piece of marble. "Where are your drawings?"

Eddie had no drawings.

"You get me a drawing, and you come back tomorrow and show me what it's going to look like."

Eddie had never sketched out his work, but he prepared one for Houser. "I took the drawing back and he was happy and gave me some pointers."

One day, Houser introduced Eddie to limestone. "Have you ever tried any of that Kansas limestone?"

"No," Eddie replied.

"Well, you should try some. It's really a pretty yellow stone, and it's easy to work with."[6]

•••

When Eddie and the other students completed the class, Houser told Eddie he wanted to speak to him. Eddie went to his office and sat down across the desk from him. Houser, a man of few words, simply said, "I want to encourage you to go to art school."[7]

"Do you think it would help me . . . ?"

"I think you should to the Institute of American Indian Arts in Santa Fe. I'll help you get in if you want to go." The IAIA is devoted to the study of contemporary Native and Alaska Native arts. As many as 112 tribes are represented on campus each year, and about 20 percent of the students are non-Native American.

Houser's suggestion came as a big surprise, for Eddie had never thought of going back to school. He knew he faced some tough decisions. He was forty years old with a wife and children. Pulling up stakes and going to the IAIA for three years would require a leap of faith into an unknown future.

When Eddie returned home, he discussed Houser's suggestion with

Vicki, and they both knew it would be a great opportunity for him. However, he decided to put the idea on hold.

During the next few months, Eddie found out everything he could about the Institute. He became convinced that he should make every effort to go there and learn as much as possible from these great art teachers. "I was surprised to learn that it was the only fine-arts institution in the nation devoted to Native American arts."

Eddie had started out drawing and painting, but studying at the feet of master sculptor Houser helped him to fall further in love with sculpture. Although he knew he loved sculpting, he soon learned that it was quite a challenge and would require a lot of hard work.

Despite some misgivings, Eddie applied to the Institute and was accepted. School officials also informed him they would grant him a scholarship. "The scholarship was really good news and would, along with my part-time jobs, help me provide for my family back home."

Eddie and Vicki agreed it would be best for her and Jennifer to stay in Caldwell, where they would be with her parents and where Jennifer was already settled in a good school. So he packed his bags, promised her he would return home once each month to see her and Jennifer, loaded his Ford pickup, and headed for a bright new world called Santa Fe.

He chose a route that would take him south into Oklahoma, across the Oklahoma Panhandle to Amarillo, Texas, then into New Mexico and down to Santa Fe. "I was on pins and needles and all kinds of questions kept going through my mind. Am I doing the right thing? Can I make it? Am I too old to be going back to school? Is this a real dream or just a pipe dream? I missed my family but really enjoyed the scenery along the way and even saw a lot of wildlife such as antelopes. That was exciting."

Eddie felt like a schoolboy again as he drove up to the Institute, but he was surprised when he saw the buildings. "They looked like old army buildings. But of course, these many years later, they have a beautiful new campus."

He pushed open the main door and walked inside. "They call me Eddie Morrison and I'm here to enroll in school," he told the lady at the front desk. She directed him to the office of the registrar, where he completed the enrollment process. The next day he went to his first class.

Throughout the next few weeks, his professors opened up new vistas to him. "Suddenly I realized how much there was to learn to become a successful sculptor and how little I knew. But I was confident that I was in the right place, so I listened very carefully to my teachers."

He smiled. "There were two or three older guys like me in the class.

The younger guys called us 'grandpas.' But it was good-natured fun and I made a lot of friends with the other aspiring artists from several other tribes."

The instructors at the Institute encouraged the students to learn to think beyond what they had ever believed they could do with their art. "They really wanted you to stretch your creative imagination to go beyond something that's like what everybody's doing."

Eddie also learned to work with different art forms, including ceramics, painting, and drawing. But he went there to study sculpting, particularly three-dimensional sculpting.

During his first year at the Institute, he learned that St. Vincent's Hospital in Santa Fe was looking for a medical technologist. He applied and was hired to work the night shift. Going to school during the day and working at night was somewhat difficult, but he knew being able to work would let him take better care of his family back in Caldwell.

The Institute required each student to lead one sunrise prayer service, in order to acquaint the other students with the culture and traditions of the various tribes.

Eddie didn't know what to do to familiarize his classmates with the Cherokee traditions. "I decided to call Crosslin Fields Smith, our Cherokee spiritual leader in Oklahoma, and ask him for help. He was very gracious and even wrote a Cherokee prayer for me to read at the service."

Crosslin Smith is called on to bless various ceremonial events and activities associated with the Cherokee Nation. Born in 1929, he said there is a "universal spirituality" given by the Great Creator that abides in all Cherokees. "Whenever you pray or meditate, do so to your inner spirit. You have his spirit in you." He added that all Native Americans are connected to the things of the past, the present, and the future and that the spirit in man never dies. "It goes from one eternity to another eternity," noted Betty Smith of AAA Native Arts.

The prayer Smith sent to Eddie began, "First, lay the wood where fire will be with ends of the logs touching end to end and the other ends pointing in the four cardinal directions. Red lady of the eternal fire, come and stand beside me with all our ancestors and give us strength." Then all those present walked around the fire seven times and sang a Cherokee song. "It was a very moving experience to be in prayer with my Native American friends from the different tribes as the sun came up over the mountains."[8]

Crosslin Smith, as the Cherokee spiritual leader, has had a profound influence on Eddie and other Cherokees as he encourages them to remember who they are and from whence they came. Following is one of Eddie's favorite encouragements that he has heard many times since childhood from the great spiritual leader, a message for all Cherokees and other Native Americans.[9]

> It is my honor to ask you during this blessing, if you can, disconnect from all people, disconnect from everything, your emotions, your feelings, your fears and likes. Blank everything out that stands as a creation. The blessing is a central blessing which is a spirit that was given to treatments. Even now, if you have some kind of affliction, or ailment, if you are doing what I'm asking you to do, it is the Creator that will heal you.
>
> Once you have succeeded, and become one with your own spirit, in that reunification you will receive a divine blessing, a divine cleansing, with the divine power so each and every one of us can make a new day every day as when we are born into this world. This is a very old and ancient tradition and is of the spirit.
>
> When you stand before your God as his creation, merge your mind, body, and soul with your spirit that lives in your body. When you succeed in becoming one with the spirit that lives in your body, that spirit, like nothing else, will make connection back to where it came from. It's called a "reunification" of your spirit with the spirit of the Creator. We use these meditations in healing for yourself. Once you receive this, you are to be happy. You are to be one with all creation. We come together in this manner as if we were standing as one people. And to be happy, you need to share that divine blessing with all of our people that have gone before us, regardless of race, creed, or color. And share that divine blessing with all the people that live in this world today.
>
> This is the most satisfying piece of work that you can do in the spiritual realm and is most satisfying to our God. And share that divine blessing with everything that's coming from the teacher and clearly from the one they call the Son of God. This is the most comprehensive and complete spiritual meditation that we can have. It comes from our ancestors; it comes from the people who made the Trail of Tears; it comes way before our people came to this North American continent.
>
> In appreciation to all of these things, we offer our traditional thanksgiving song. And this song, no one can understand the sounds that are made. It is designed for only the God to understand. This will complete our divine blessing.
>
> Because of your original ancient law even to all people, we come to stand before you because of that ancient law, our spiritual law written to all people. We come to commune with you today by the spirit that you gave us. Amen.

Being around the students from other tribes such as the Pueblo, Apache, and Navajo helped Eddie develop a great respect for Native Americans everywhere. "Seeing their traditions and culture—and observing their works of art at the Institute—was very enlightening and caused my mind to explode with creative ideas. We studied everything from the history of Native American art to Native American astronomy and had hands-on instruction in three-dimensional sculpturing and other disciplines. These were some of the finest teachers in the world, and on workdays they would watch us and give us personal attention with our work."

Eddie majored in three-dimensional art. "It is art that you can walk around and see the whole, as compared to a painting where you only see one side."

In one class, the students would critique one another's work. "Talk about critics! I mean at times it got brutal, and some days I would walk out of the class feeling pretty low because of the way my work was criticized." But he knew it was not personal and vowed to keep going, regardless of what any of the other students thought of his work.

Although the students were free to develop their art around any Native American themes and legends, Eddie concentrated on those relating to the Cherokees. "I did one sculpture I called the *Ice Man and the Fire* and another I called the *Great Mystic Hawk*, both based on stories of great hunters."

The students went on several field trips to Indian country in northern Arizona and New Mexico, where Eddie learned a lot about other Indian cultures and was fascinated by them. "We visited the Hopi Indian mesas in Arizona." While there, the students witnessed one of the golden twilights that transfigures the mesas and saw a traditional Hopi kachina.

The kachina is an important dance ritual of the Hopi Indians. Kachinas are believed to be supernatural beings that, during a certain time of the year, visit the Hopi villages to form a link between the Indians and the gods. The "dolls" called kachinas are actually religious icons carved from cottonwood roots and painted to look like figures from Hopi mythology. They are also believed to be the spirits of both living things and ancestors who become a part of nature and, hence, have control over nature.

"I really have a lot of respect for the Hopi Indians," Eddie said. "The mesas are a thousand years old and the Hopis still live high up on the top. It's amazing how they were able to build their homes up there, for it's such a steep road all the way up the side of the mountain. Some historians believe they built their homes on the mesa for protection from enemies."

The teachers at the Institute required each student to do a painting or carving during the field trips. When they visited the mesas, Eddie painted one of the old Hopi villages.

The students also visited Chaco Canyon in northwestern New Mexico, between Farmington and Albuquerque. It was home to the ancestors of today's Pueblo Indians until about 850 A.D., when they suddenly disappeared.

What became of these people remains a mystery, and Eddie is curious about them to this day. "They were called the 'Ancient Ones' and no one knows exactly what happened to them."

Eddie discovered something very interesting about these "Ancient Ones." He believes that their culture was based on astronomy, for they had petroglyphs of the moon, winter and summer solstices, and spring equinox. "I wish we had the answers to the meaning of all of those drawings, for they are very interesting."

Even today, Eddie remembers the old kivas of Chaco Canyon, where the early Indians held their religious ceremonies. "We climbed down a ladder into the underground room where the kivas were located. It was a very moving experience, and I could almost see the Indians doing their ceremonial dance, drums beating, fires burning, and the elders sitting around on benches chanting."

After three years of intense study, Eddie graduated from the Institute in 1993. During the graduation ceremony, the faculty named him the best student in the three-dimensional arts department. "It was a great honor, and I was encouraged that the faculty members saw some merit in my work. I will always be grateful to them for that." Years after Eddie graduated, the Institute became a four-year school.

The graduation ceremony was unique and colorful. The graduates wore their individual tribe's native regalia as they entered the Greer Garson Theater to the sounds of singing and drumming by the Heartbeat Singers of Taos, New Mexico. The theater is located on the campus, and officials named it in honor a movie star of an earlier generation.

Eddie didn't have any traditional Indian clothing and really didn't know what to wear. "But I came up with the idea of wearing a moose-skin vest with a red-tailed-hawk feather on it. Some of my classmates—Apaches, Navajos, Hopis, and others—wore some really colorful costumes."

Reflecting on his three years at the Institute, he said, "I think it helped me to be an older student. I was able to concentrate more than I would have when I was young."[10]

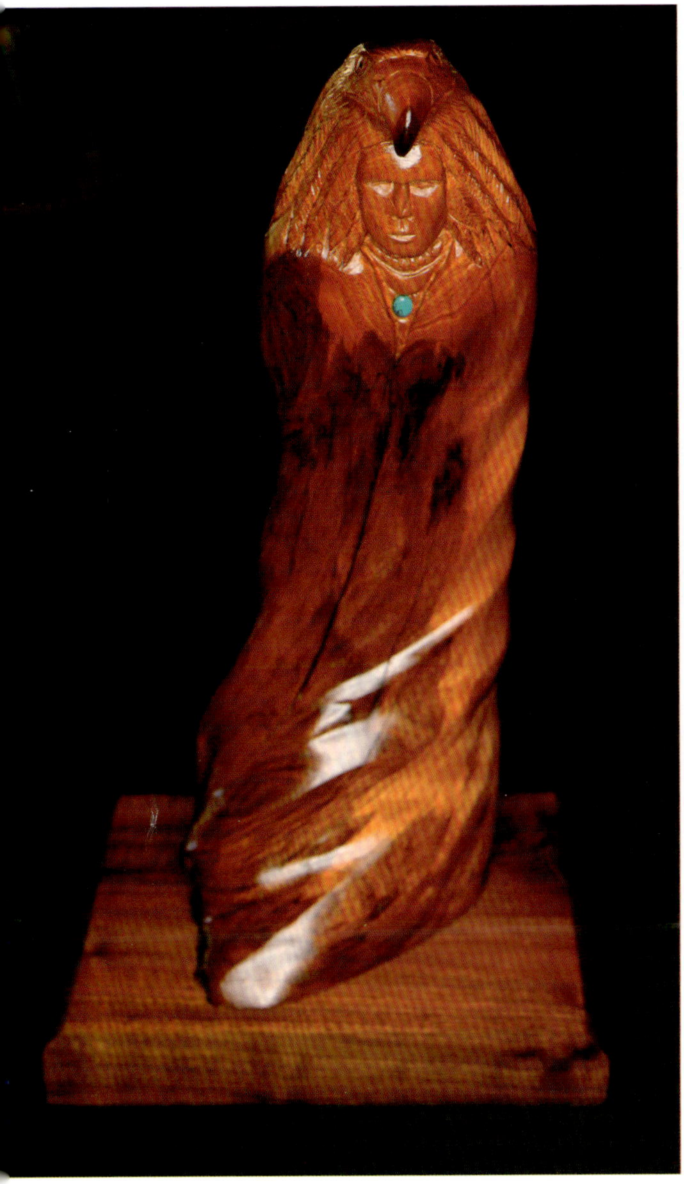

Caped Native American, carved from cedar

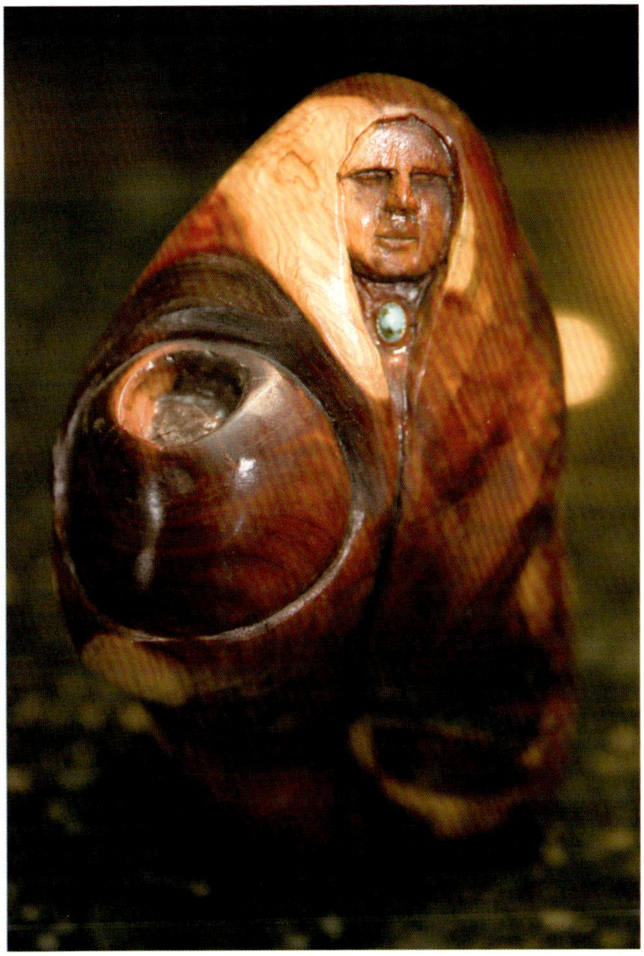

Cherokee woman carrying pottery, carved from cedar with turquoise around her neck (Photograph by Brandon Scott)

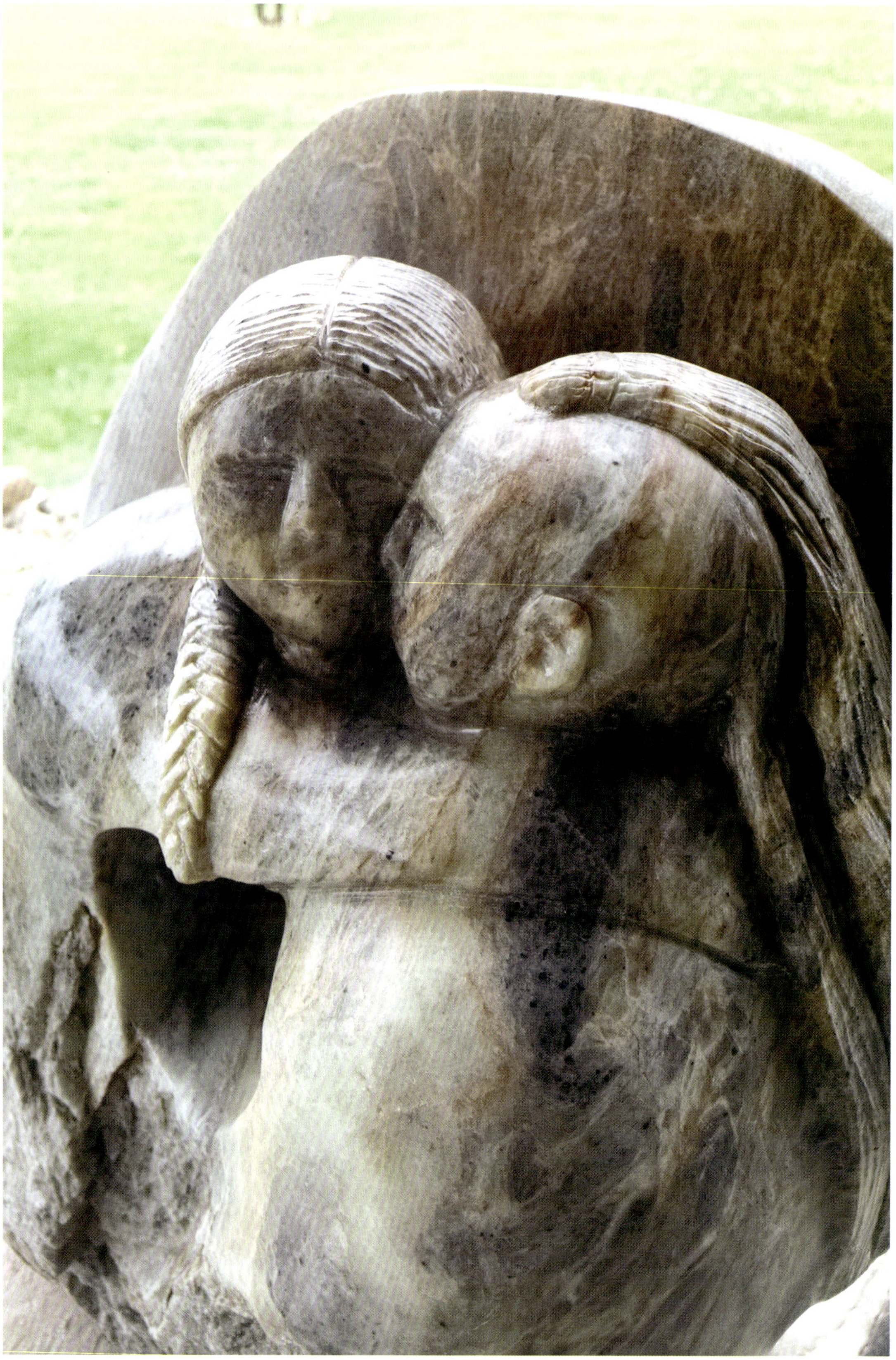

Indian warrior and his woman, carved from British Columbia steatite

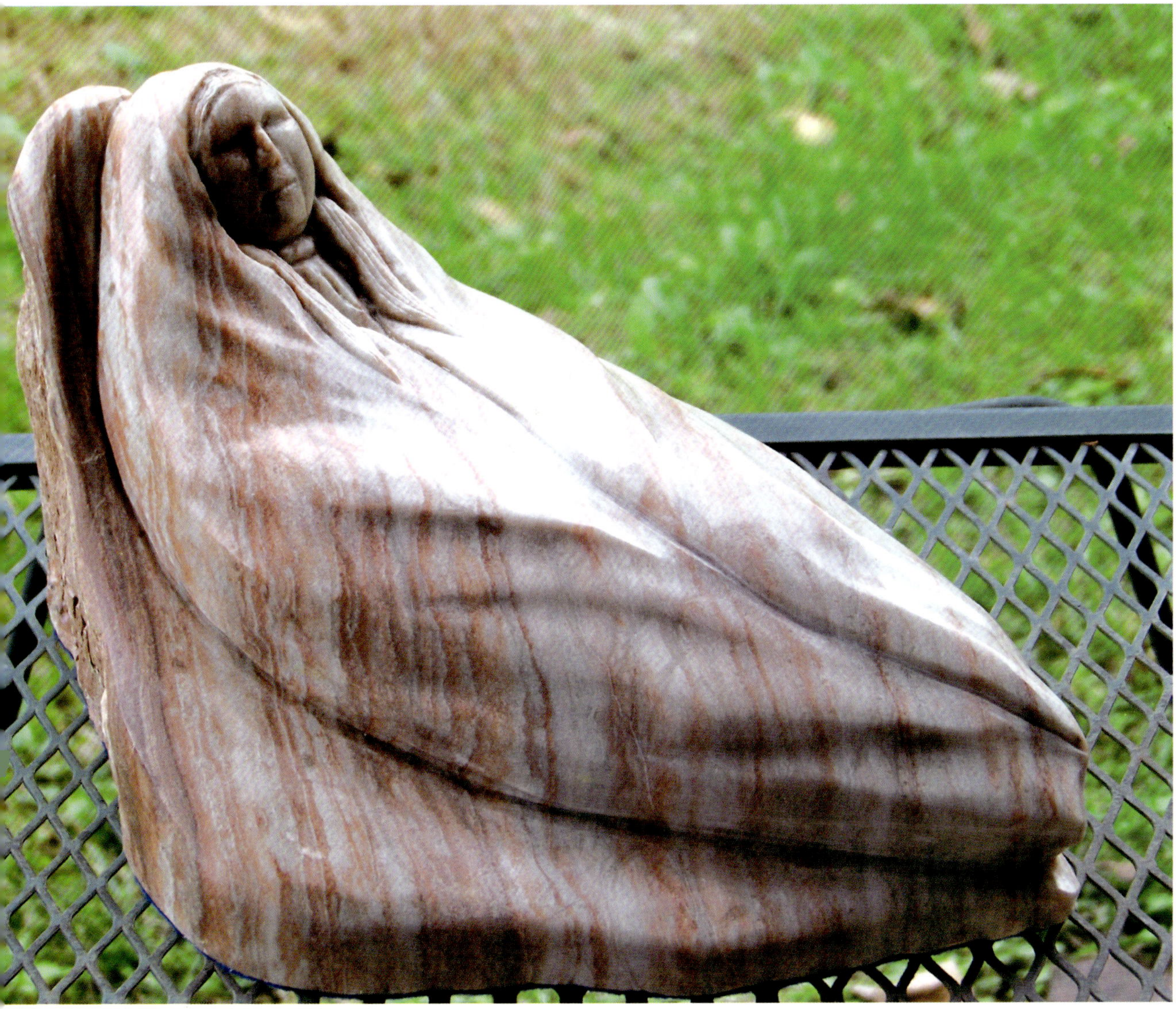

Reclining Woman, *carved from alabaster*

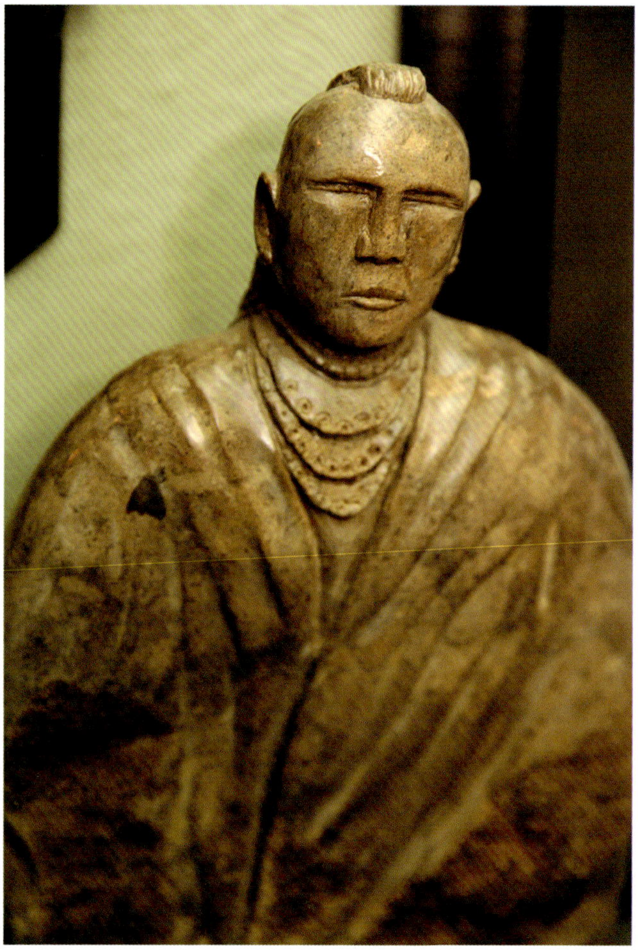

Ancient Cherokee Warrior, *carved from Oklahoma limestone* (Photograph by Brandon Scott)

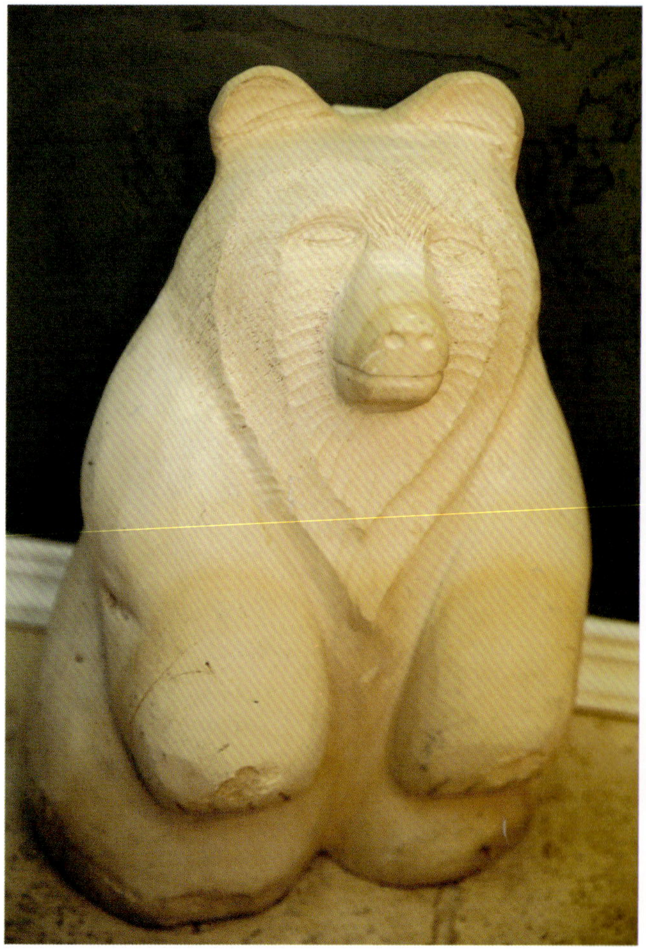

Bear, carved from Kansas limestone (Photograph by Brandon Scott)

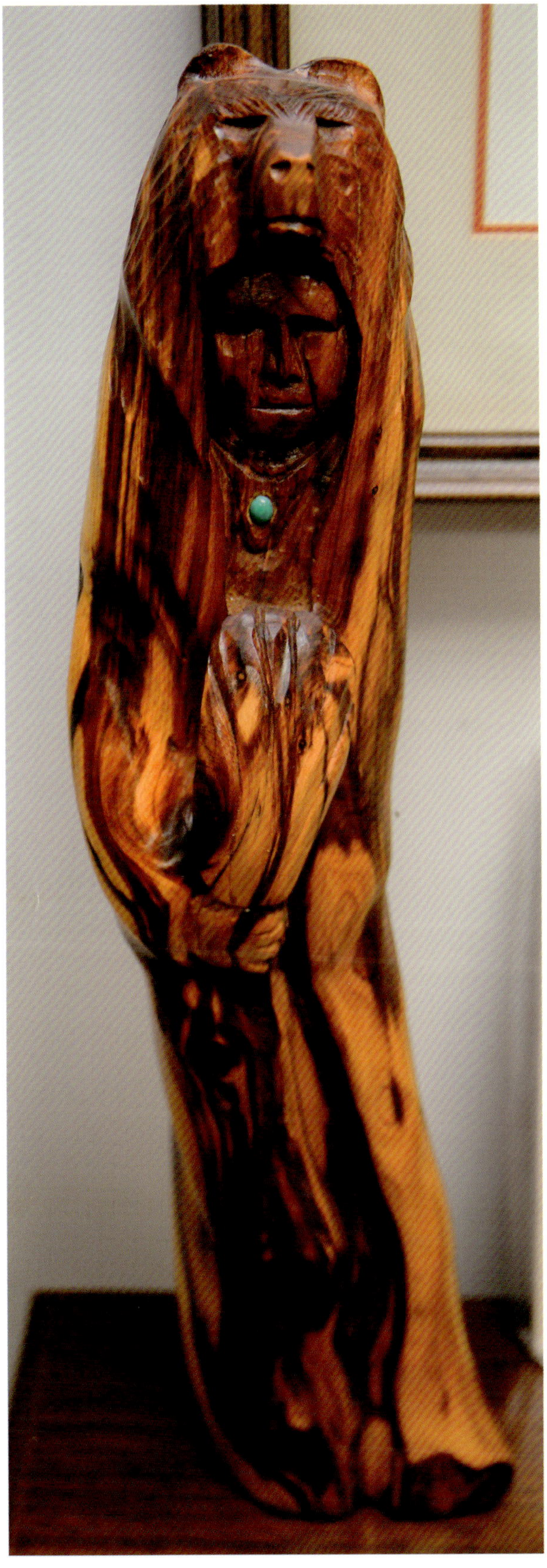

Bear-caped Cherokee warrior, carved from cedar

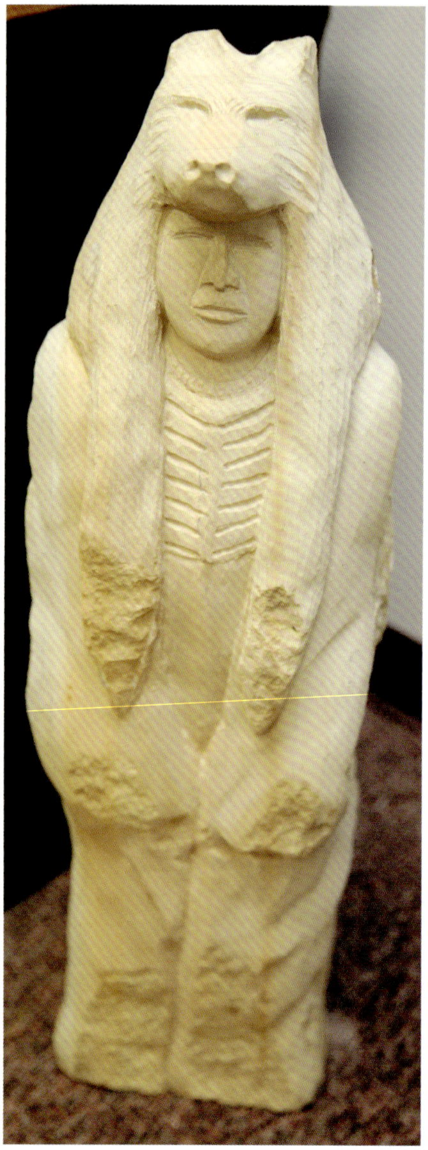

Wolf-caped man, carved from Kansas limestone (Photograph by Brandon Scott)

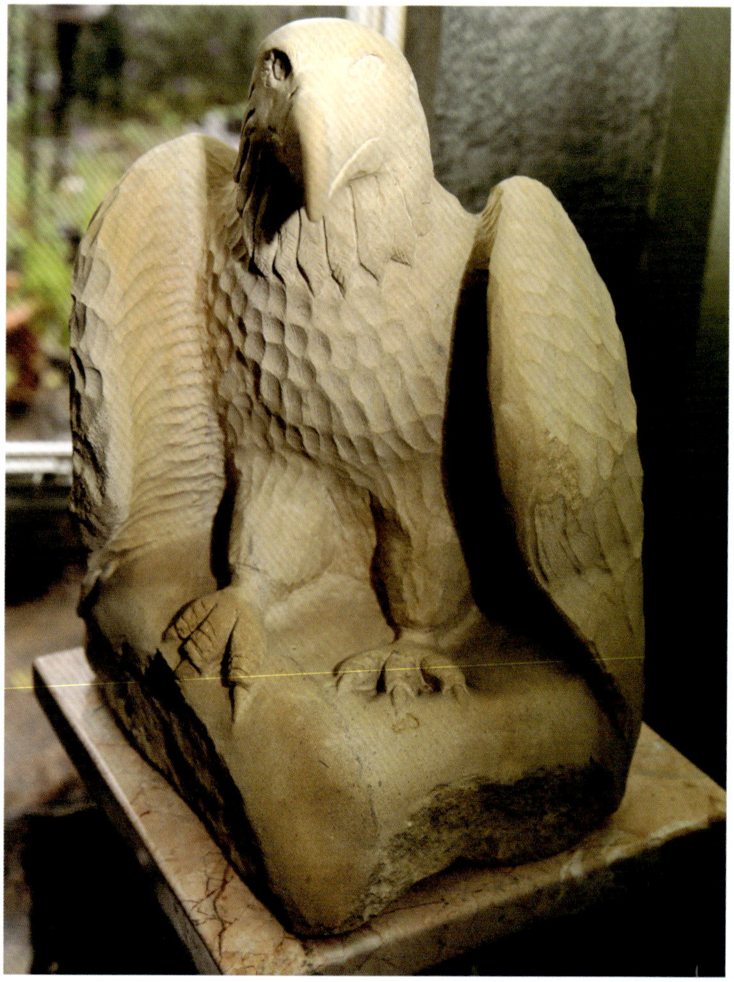

Eagle, carved from Kansas limestone (Photograph by Brandon Scott)

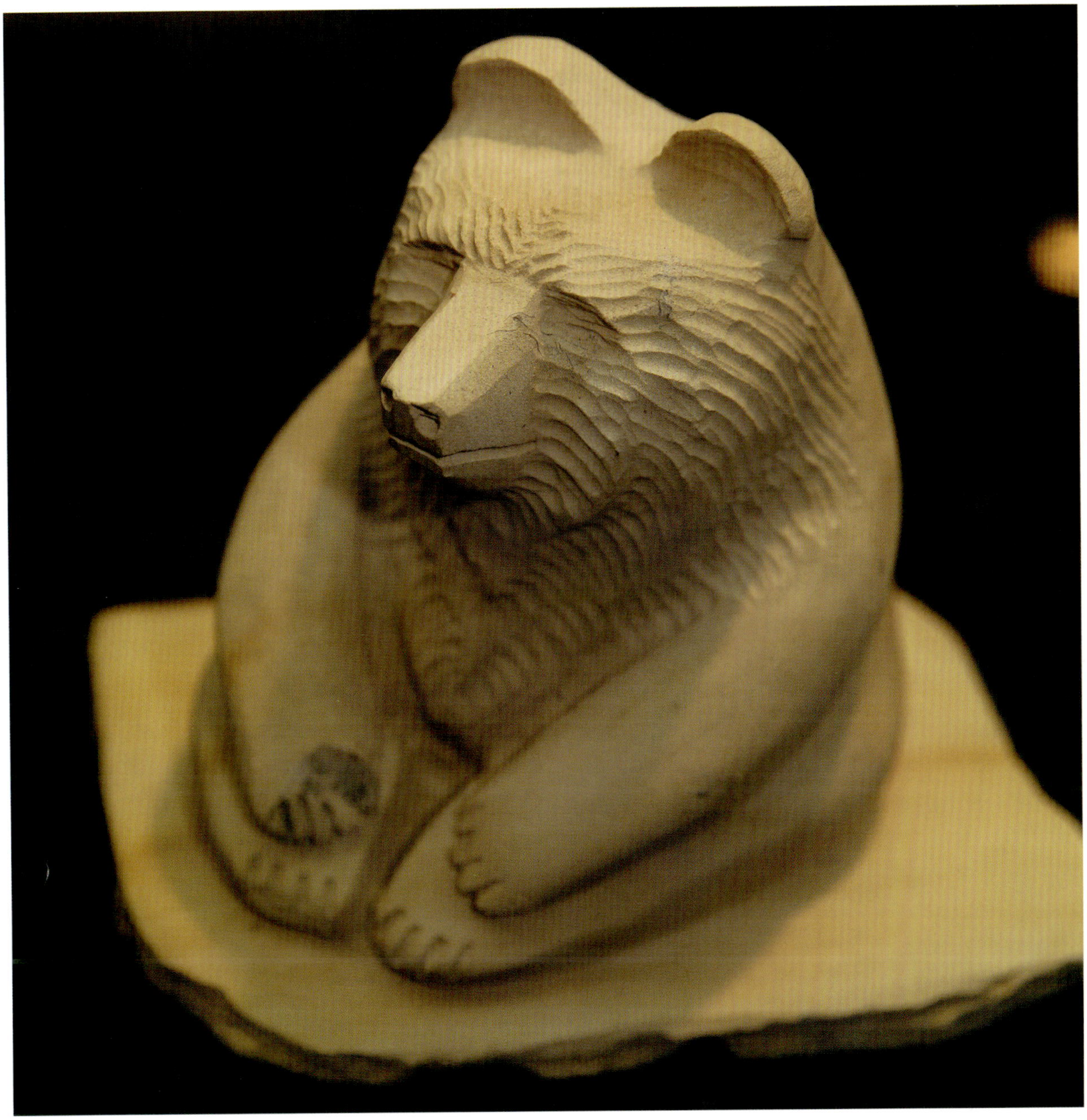

Sitting bear, carved from Kansas limestone (Photograph by Brandon Scott)

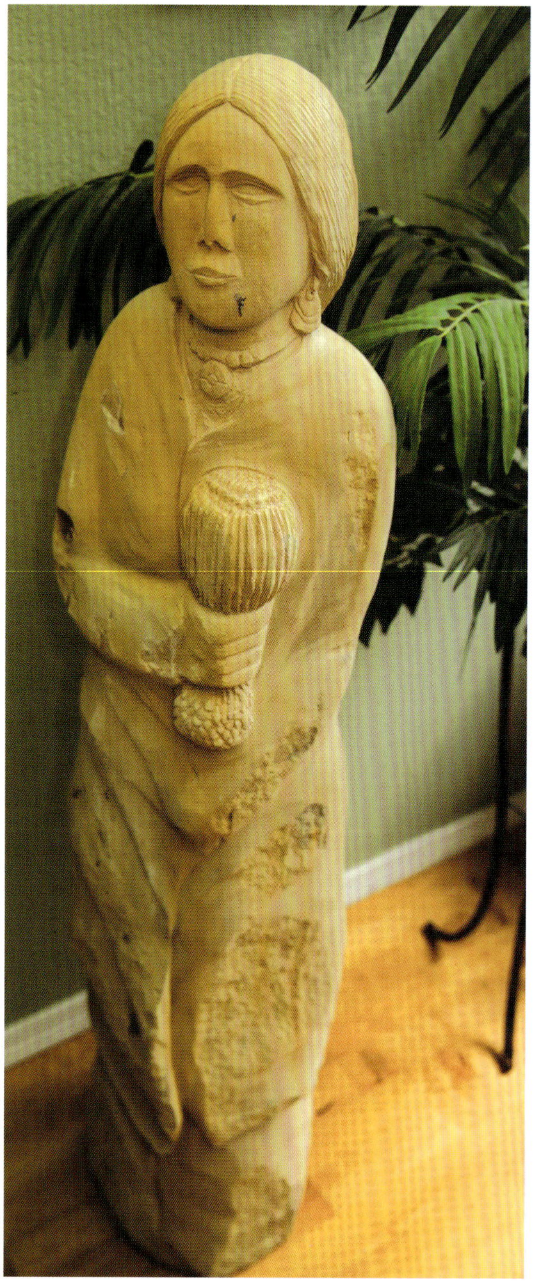

Limestone sculpture of a Native American woman holding wild onions (Photograph by Brandon Scott)

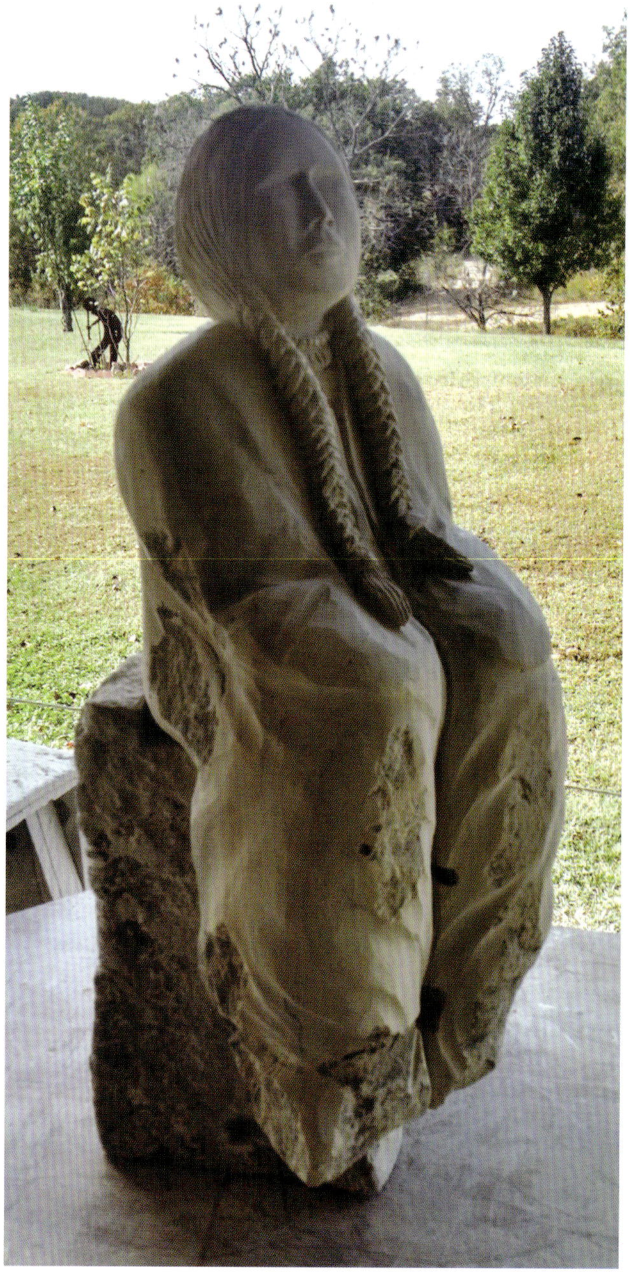

Limestone sitting piece from Jim Locke's collection (Photograph by Brandon Scott)

Chapter Five

The Opera House

After graduating from the Institute, Eddie was anxious to return to his family in Caldwell, and he knew he was ready to begin working full time as an artist. He packed his few belongings in his Ford pickup and left Santa Fe for the 500-mile trip home.

As he drove along the highway, he realized it had been a great privilege to attend the Institute. "I knew I would always remember the students, faculty, field trips, and hands-on training where I had the privilege of studying the art of sculpture from some of the best teachers in the world."

In Caldwell, he decided it was time to take a great leap of faith and open a gallery and studio. There he could pursue his passion for art, a passion that had been latent for years but now permeated his soul.

Today, however, he admits that he was apprehensive about going into business for himself and hoped he wasn't just chasing a rainbow through the rain. He knew there was some risk involved, but he wanted a gallery where he could display his art—and that of other artists—and a studio where he could work. He decided Caldwell would be a good place to start.

As he looked around the city for a location, he learned that the once-famous Opera House on Main Street was vacant. It was a two-story, stucco-over-brick building and had been the center of entertainment in Caldwell in its day.[1]

Eddie couldn't wait to take a look at the old place. He hoped it was exactly what he was looking for. "The old Opera House was perfect. The way it was arranged, I could display my artwork in the front window. There was an unfinished basement with a dirt floor."

New dreams began to take wing in Eddie's imagination. He decided the basement would be a perfect place to do the dusty carving, sawing, and chipping with a chisel. There was also a work area in the back where he could do his finishing work.[2]

Eddie leased the Opera House and displayed a 300-pound marble sculpture he named *A Tribute to Endangered Species* in the front window. He carved it out of Yule Marble, found only in rock quarries in the Yule Creek Valley in Colorado. It is the same marble used for the Lincoln Memorial and the Tomb of the Unknown Soldier in Washington, D.C.

During a lengthy interview with newspaper reporter Phyllis Griekspoor of the *Wichita Eagle,* Eddie said the old Opera House was ideal for his work and discussed the process in detail. "It's just plain dirty work," he said as he used a power drill on a stone carving that, when finished, would depict an old Indian man giving a prayer of thanks for a basket of herbs he was holding.[3]

He shared a great deal with the reporter about his personal feelings toward his work. "Creativity is still truly a mystery to me. Sometimes when I do a piece and then stand back and look at it, it seems that it just comes from somewhere inside me."[4]

The people of Caldwell were quite curious about the new art gallery in the old Opera House. "But they were nice to me and respectful and I had many wonderful friends there and still do today. It just took them awhile to warm up to me."

Some of Eddie's experiences with the good people of Caldwell were quite comical. "When I started working on my art pieces, a lot of people did not understand exactly what I was doing. They had never seen a sculptor at work. One day an old gentleman came into the shop, walked back to the studio, and saw me working on a piece of limestone. He shook his head and said, 'You need to get a real job.'"

Few locals visited the gallery. But Eddie hosted a Christmas reception there each year. "That's when most of the people would come—to get free cookies and some other treats. However, my friend Damon Weber, the editor of the *Caldwell Messenger,* wrote several good articles about my gallery and my work."

Weber also commissioned Eddie to carve his and his wife's gravestone out of Kansas limestone. "It was a very unusual carving, for he wanted a Celtic cross design on one side of the monument and Cherokee designs on the other."

Eddie did sell a few pieces to local residents. "The telephone company purchased an alabaster carving I called the *Keeper of the Fire* and displayed it in the lobby of their office building. The Wichita Indian Museum purchased a limestone carving of an Indian man, and a lady in Caldwell bought a large cedar relief carving and gave it to the Border Queen Museum in Caldwell. It was a carving of the Oklahoma land run."

In this 1889 event, Indian lands were taken away by the government and given to others. Eddie's carving depicts the people on their horses lining up on the Cherokee Strip and four Indians watching them take their land away.

While in Caldwell, Eddie carved some pieces that became quite famous. One, from a large piece of walnut, depicted the Trail of Tears, the horrific forced march of the Cherokee people from their homeland in Georgia to Indian Territory. Thousands died from starvation, disease, and freezing weather during the march as they faced all of the sickening contrasts and diabolical ironies of life under government oppression.[5]

Eddie did another relief in red cedar for Caldwell's celebration of the centennial "Run for the Cherokee Strip," which commemorated the event that changed Oklahoma from Indian Territory to an area open to white settlement.

In Caldwell, he developed his strong work ethic, which has served him well through the years. "I can lose myself for hours when I'm working. Sometimes I look at the clock and discover the whole day has gone by."

The Caldwell years also firmly established him as an artist of merit, as galleries in other states called him and asked to display his art. Also, collectors purchased his works for exhibit at the National Museum of the American Indian in New York City, at Yosemite National Park, and in the Department of the Interior in Washington, D.C., among others.[6] The National Museum of the American Indian, established in 1989, is located in the Old Customs House, across the street from Battery Park in Manhattan.

Also during Eddie's Opera House days, the international market first opened for him, when a gallery in Australia asked to display his works. "Although I had some success in art shows and galleries here in this land, I had never even dreamed of the possibility of selling my work in a foreign land."

In time, the people of Caldwell learned to love Eddie and appreciate his work. "That meant a lot to me and made me feel that at long last I had been accepted by the people there."

While living and working in Caldwell, unfortunate circumstances led to the breakup of Eddie's marriage to Vicki. After that, he decided to close the Opera House gallery and move back to Tahlequah. He and Vicki have remained friends through the years.

After returning to Tahlequah, Eddie received a call from a lady in Caldwell by the name of Pat Barrett. She asked him to do a bas relief in natural limestone as a memorial to her late husband, Richard Barrett, who was a great lover of history, particularly related to Caldwell and the surrounding area.

Eddie agreed to do the monument but knew he had to find a four-foot stone and have it cut to his specifications. He located it in Sylvan, Kansas, and it weighed 1,600 pounds. He hauled it back to his studio in Tahlequah in the bed of his pickup.

Since it was the heaviest piece of limestone he had ever worked with, Eddie called several friends to help him unload it. "We decided to use pipes as rollers. So we lifted the edge of the stone, placed the pipes underneath, and then rolled it onto a platform and into the studio."[7]

Then he went to work. "I sketched all the scenes on the studio wall. I called the work *Those Who Came Before*. It took me ten months to complete the monument. That was the longest I had ever worked on any piece of art, but it was well worth the time and I'm proud of it to this day."

The monument was a tribute to both the native people of the area and the white pioneers who settled the territory. Since Caldwell was on the legendary Chisholm Trail, Eddie carved a bust of Jesse Chisholm, for whom the trail is named, in the center of the memorial. "To me, Jesse Chisholm—who was half-Cherokee—is a symbol of the blending of cultures, both because of his mixed race and because of his connection with the trail that brought the cattle industry north to this area," Eddie told Griekspoor.

The finished sculpture, one of the most ambitious projects he had ever undertaken, depicted early settlers, Native Americans, buffalos, birds, and a motif of eagle wings, from the biblical passage "they shall soar on wings like eagles." At the bottom right is a buffalo, and at the bottom left, a longhorn steer. Subtle shadings of eagle wing rise from either side of the bust of Chisholm, to above the family images.

The monument depicted the variety of cultures that, through the years, had occupied and influenced Caldwell and the surrounding area. A representative of the city would point out, "Each group, from Native Americans to early pioneers, farmers, and adventurers, has shared the same land, work ethic, concern for family, and belief in divine influence. An underlying theme is the common view that our spirits, our prayers, and our hopes are carried on the wings of a soaring eagle."

Eddie has often used images of eagles, for he appreciates the symbolism and says the eagle is sacred to both white and Indian cultures. "The white culture reveres the eagle as a symbol of freedom, and the Indian culture reveres the eagle as a bearer of prayers and messages to the Creator. That's why I carved the subtle eagle wings, to create paths to the heavens from both sides."[8]

Once finished, Eddie had another problem. How was he going to get the large stone out of his studio and back onto the bed of his pickup? "Getting it out of the studio was the hard part. It was scary. A friend brought his forklift to help me load the monument. It was large and in a tight spot. So it was really tricky getting it out of there without breaking it. But we finally got it out and loaded on a trailer and I headed for Caldwell."[9]

The *Eagle* article captured the essence and importance of Eddie's work as he perfected his art on the long road to national acclaim. It also provided a detailed description of *Those Who Came Before* and said it was one of his best pieces. "The relief is done in storytelling style of a traditional petro glyph (a carving or an inscription on a rock) and features a white pioneer family at the top left and a Native American family and its traditional dwellings, teepees, and a Wichita grass house at the top right."

The *Eagle* reporter noted that Eddie honors both the Native American people and the white pioneers in his works, for he believes they have much in common. "They were all very spiritual people," Eddie said. "All those who lived through those times helped build a future and it was not an easy time for anyone."

Griekspoor wrote that Eddie "attempts to meld traditional art forms and modern techniques into a work that shares contemporary stories and ideas with traditional stories and methodology." The article further noted that he does not even try to be historically accurate in every detail of clothing, headdress, or culture. He said, "The main thing to me is to tell the story, to preserve the major ideas of the culture. I like to think that the general image can relate to far more people than it would if I narrowed it to very specific segments of people."

Eddie also told the reporter that he saw no value in attempting to be absolutely true to the art techniques of a time long past. He sought to create "a new generation and a new time that is Native American art" and had no trouble using modern tools and methods. He felt this showed progress in Native American art.

When the Cherokees first arrived in Indian Territory, Eddie says they discovered a rugged, empty land. A bad wind blew and brought memories of their lost homelands. The Cherokees, however, "became living proof that the flames of freedom may burn low but they never die."

Pat Barrett gave the monument to the city of Caldwell and asked that it be placed on Highway 81 on the border between Oklahoma and Kansas, along the route of the legendary Chisholm Trail.

It was an exciting day for Eddie when dozens of people gathered out on Highway 81 at the Oklahoma-Kansas border to dedicate the memorial. "There were members of the historic Chisholm family along with state and local officials. I felt a lot of satisfaction being able to record an important time in history through my work. The Chisholm family gave me some colorful Indian blankets to remember the great event."[10]

The monument is still there today.

•••

Eddie will always remember Caldwell and the days he dared to dream, but he was glad to be back in Tahlequah. Today northeastern Oklahoma and the Tahlequah area are known as Green Country, and Eddie thinks it is the most beautiful place on earth. "There's nothing like Tahlequah, surrounded by the colorful foothills of the Ozark Mountains with crystal-clear creeks and rivers, rolling hills, and beautiful lakes."

Eddie, who feels an affinity with nature, looks forward each year to the beautiful wildflowers waving in the wind, bringing the promise of spring as winter fades away.

In 2001, while living in Tahlequah, Eddie often thought of Faye Hammons, his high-school girlfriend, and wondered what had become of her. One day by chance he met her brother Jerry and asked about her. "He told me she was still living in Tahlequah and she was single. That was very interesting news."

Eddie decided to give her a call to renew their long-lost acquaintance. "I called her at her beauty shop and said I wanted to see her, but she told me no."

However, he was persistent and phoned her again the next day.

"Can we go get a hamburger?

"No."

He didn't call her again for some time, but on Thanksgiving he called her mother and asked for Faye's home phone number. Faye had asked her mother not to give that out to anyone, but she gave it to Eddie.

When her mother told her that Eddie had called and she had given him her phone number, Faye knew he wasn't going to give up. So she decided to call him.

"When he answered and found out it was me, he said, 'I thought you were history.' Again he asked if he could come by my house and I said, 'Come on over.'"[11]

That was the beginning of the renaissance of their romance. Faye enjoyed his company. "He was kind and generous and really affectionate toward me. And he was the same old Eddie, sometimes very reserved and quiet and other times laughing and telling jokes."

After a whirlwind romance, Eddie asked Faye to marry him and she said yes. It was a happy time for both of them. "Eddie and I had found one another again after all those years and now we looked forward to being together as husband and wife."

The wedding was held in the historic Indian Methodist Church on Seneca Street in Tahlequah. The church was filled with family members and a host of friends who loved Faye and Eddie and wanted to share in the happy occasion.

Eddie is proud that he and Faye had two ceremonies. "We had a traditional Cherokee ceremony performed by two ministers, Wynema Smith and Ray Keener. Keener was an old-time Cherokee Methodist preacher. After the traditional ceremony, Francine Biggoose conducted the ceremony in English." Biggoose, a member of the Ponca Indian tribe, is an ordained Methodist minister.

Eddie and Faye said it was a happy and memorable wedding. The traditional ceremony began with Cherokee hymns sung by the Cherokee choir. After the music, Eddie stood at the altar, wearing a white shirt with an eagle feather and holding a basket with a smoked turkey leg. Faye entered with a basket of fruit, which was replaced by a flower bouquet embellished with an eagle feather that Eddie had given her. The turkey represented the fact that Eddie would provide for his wife and the fruit that Faye would prepare food for her husband.

Next, the couple, wrapped together in a blanket, danced counterclockwise around burning cedar and tobacco seven times, while the choir sang Cherokee songs. Then they presented each other with beaded necklaces—Eddie's turquoise with white and Faye's white with turquoise—symbolizing their bond.

The Cherokee Nation issued the marriage license.

Following the traditional Cherokee ceremony, Reverend Biggoose officiated the Christian wedding. Attending Eddie were grandsons Marcus and Josh Glass, and the ring bearers were Eddie's grandson Jacob Morrison and Faye's grandson Colton Cox. Faye's granddaughter Sierra Cox was the flower girl. The choir, Reverend Smith, and Sierra Cox wore traditional "tear" dresses, the official tribal dresses worn by women of the Cherokee Nation.

Eddie and Faye still attend this Methodist church. The services are in English, but some of the people, when asked to pray, do so in Cherokee. They conduct an all-Cherokee service once a month. Faye is also the director of the Cherokee Adult Choir, made up of both Protestant and Catholic singers.

Faye is in awe of Eddie's artistic talent. "He never even had any interest in art when I knew him back in high school. But now I see his great talent and I am amazed."

She loves to travel with him to art shows. "Once we were on our way to Denver, Colorado, for the Indian Arts and Crafts Association show, and when we passed through Medford, Oklahoma, Eddie told me he wanted to stop and take care of some business at the local bank."

"What kind of business is he talking about?" she wondered.

She soon found out. "We had a four-foot sculpture in the back of the pickup. It was of a young Indian girl with long black hair, like one of the young ladies in the Methodist church where Eddie and I worship."

Faye didn't know that the banker was Eddie's friend and, through the years, had purchased several of his works. While they were talking in the bank that day, the banker asked him if he had any other pieces of art for sale. "Eddie told him about the sculpture of the Indian girl with the long black hair."

"How much do you want for it?" the banker asked.

"Three thousand dollars."

"I'll take it."

Faye said the banker told Eddie he would call a moving company to come by the bank and unload the sculpture.

When Eddie told Faye how much the banker paid for the piece before he even looked at it, her jaw dropped and she shook her head in disbelief. "Three thousand dollars! That's a lot of money!" But she knew that the piece was worth it, because her husband put his heart and soul into the beautiful work of art.

Faye always respects Eddie's desire to be alone when he is working in his studio so he can concentrate solely on his work. "When he gets started on a new sculpture, he really gets into it and there's no stopping him."

She's always delighted when she sees his finished work. "I'm amazed how he can see the finished work in his mind before he even begins and wants to get it through his hands and onto the stone. I love his work and would like to keep everything he does, for each one of them is so special. But I know that is impossible."

One of the great desires of her heart is to give Eddie moral support, whether in the home, at a faraway art show, or during a newspaper or television interview. "There's something about Eddie that would make the Cherokee people very proud of him. Everywhere we go, Eddie is a proud ambassador for the Cherokee people, and I'm honored I get to be a part of it."

Eddie remembers when his dreams of working with different kinds of art kept stirring in his heart. His work evolved from pen-and-inks and acrylics to wood and stone carving. "I never quite felt comfortable with my pen-and-inks and acrylic paintings. It seemed like I was struggling to complete them. I always liked wood and stone, so I decided to start carving and maybe even try my hand at a few sculptures."

In the mid-1980s, there was a dramatic change of direction in his life and his work. "I sharpened my pocketknife, picked up a piece of peach wood, and started carving. It felt natural."

An early attempt at carving didn't work out too well for him. He cut off his finger and the doctor had to sew it back on. "The cut was very painful and it set me back for a few days, but before long the finger healed and I went back to work carving. I soon realized how much I enjoyed it. I would look at one of my pieces and stand back and admire it and ask myself, 'Did I really do that?'"

Working with his hands came naturally for Eddie. Most of his life, he had lived around Indian people who made things with their hands. "Even when I was growing up, I would go to art shows and see beautiful things people had made and always dreamed of creating beautiful works of my own."

When Eddie was in grade school and living with his grandmother, her sister Clyde would come to visit her on Ward Street. "She was just an old Cherokee woman who lived over in the hills near Stillwell. While she would be visiting with Grandma, she would draw pictures. I was just fascinated with her drawings. I mean, her drawings of panthers and other animals were so realistic, and she'd do them with pencil."

Eddie wishes he had kept some of his aunt Clyde's drawings. "If she hadn't been just an elderly Indian woman that nobody had ever heard of, she could have become a famous artist. I wish I had kept some of her drawings, for she had a wonderful gift. Grandma and her sister Clyde were both great artists. Grandma always crocheted and made quilts. I used to watch her and see all those intricate designs that she could create with that little needle. She came up with the most beautiful designs."

Eddie remembers being overwhelmed by a desire to learn more about art. He started reading every book he could find on carvings and sculpture, and he experimented with stone work. The more he read, the more convinced he became that there was a great big wonderful world of art somewhere out there, just waiting for him.

Chapter Six

On the Road

Being a graduate of the most prestigious Indian art school in America opened a lot of doors for Eddie. People learned that the faculty at the Institute had named him the outstanding student in the three-dimensional arts, and they were curious about his work. "It started slow, but before long I was receiving invitations to markets and galleries all across the country. It was a big door that opened, but at the time I wasn't exactly sure what to do with all that I had learned or with all the opportunities that were before me."[1]

When Eddie started going to art shows trying to sell his work, he didn't have a lot of self-confidence. During the early days, he had some wild experiences. "There was a little art show in Grove, Oklahoma, and I took my six-year-old daughter Monica with me. I had an old Ford pickup truck with a camper shell on the back. I used it to haul my art to the various shows."

Since he couldn't afford to stay in a motel, he and Monica slept on cots in the back of the pickup. "One night there was a really bad storm with thunder and lightning. The wind was howling and the camper shell was rocking back and forth. I thought the wind was going to blow it off the truck."

Later Eddie told his friends how scared he was that night. "I thought we might get blown away by that storm."

That same year, organizers of the Indian Summer Festival in Milwaukee, Wisconsin, invited Eddie to show his art. He had heard that large crowds of people attended. Wisconsin is home to eleven tribes, the greatest number east of the Mississippi River, and the Indian Summer Festival is the largest Native American festival in the United States. It presents demonstrations of beadwork, finger weaving, bow and arrow making, pottery, carving, basket weaving, and more.

Eddie said, "They also asked me to give a demonstration of woodcarving. The people would gather around and watch me as I carved a piece of cedar. They seemed to really enjoy the demonstration."

Woodcarving is a traditional Cherokee craft. Originally, the objects included domestic utensils, such as ladles, spoons, and dough trays. Pipes carved from rhododendron root, with natural and abstract animal and human forms rendered in full relief, as well as ceremonial wood masks also became popular in the tourist trade.

When he was going to various art shows, Eddie almost exclusively used cedar for his carvings. "It is the most sacred of all woods and often is used in Cherokee religious ceremonies. The distinguishing colors of red and white set it off from all others. Cherokee historians believe cedar wood was considered so sacred that in ancient Cherokee days it was used to carry the honored dead."

One day while Eddie was giving a woodcarving demonstration at the Milwaukee festival, a stranger approached his table and watched with rapt attention. "I had my raw materials there on a table and my tools, and all of a sudden this stranger came by my work table and began watching me work. I didn't have any idea who he was. Suddenly he spoke to me in a foreign language I didn't understand. But there was a young lady with him who spoke his language, and she explained he was a famous Russian painter from St. Petersburg and was showing his work at the art show."

From that time forward, Eddie and the Russian visited each day, discussed their own art forms, and became friends. The Russian seemed very interested in Eddie's carving style. He wanted to know what kind of wood Eddie was using.

"I told him it was cedar, and he watched me carve for awhile and then asked me if he could carve something. I told him he could. He carved a piece that looked like a Russian lady wearing a headdress and signed it and gave it to me. I consider it a treasure."

Eddie gave the Russian artist a woodcarving of a robed figure. "I chiseled a woodcarving out of cedar and gave it to him to take back to Russia. It was worth the trip to Milwaukee just to meet the Russian artist. The thought that one of my carvings was going all the way to St. Petersburg, Russia, was quite exciting."

Although Eddie enjoyed the festival and particularly meeting the Russian artist, one night there was a fierce storm that could have cost him his life. "The festival staff had erected what looked like tents fastened to poles, covering each artist's display. One night a storm with high winds blew the tent down on me. I couldn't find a way to get out from under it, but some of the other artists cleared the debris away and rescued me. Thankfully, I was not injured."

While on the road doing art shows in various other states, Eddie met some very interesting people. "During a show in Denver, a very attractive lady came by my booth and spent a lot of time looking over my art. Later she reached out to shake my hand."

She said, "My name is Sandy Chapin. Perhaps you've heard of my husband, Harry Chapin, who recorded 'Cat's in the Cradle'?"

Eddie tried to answer her, but he was so startled that the words didn't come easily. Finally he replied, "I'm glad to know you and I love the song, and your husband, Harry Chapin, was a great singer."

American singer-songwriter Harry Chapin (1942-81) had a number-one hit with "Cat's in the Cradle." In 1966, Sandy Cashmere, a New York socialite nine years older than him, called him asking for music lessons. They married in 1968.

Sandy continued to speak as she closely examined Eddie's work. "I own a gallery in Long Island, and I want to invite you to come to New York to do a show."

Eddie didn't know what to say. He had never done a big art show, and New York was far away.

"I will pay your way and pay for shipping your art to New York."

"Well, I'm honored you want to show my work."

"Then you'll do the show for me?"

"Yes, I will do the show."

Eddie was thankful for his good fortune and believed that his career had taken a giant step forward, courtesy of Sandy Chapin.

"On the flight to JFK International in New York City, I kept thinking, 'Man, this is just unbelievable. A poor Cherokee from Tahlequah is on his way to an art show in New York, and it's my art show.'"

During the flight, Eddie kept softly singing the words of "Cat's in the Cradle": "And the cat's in the cradle and the silver spoon, little boy blue, and the man in the moon." The man in the seat next to him must have wondered why he kept repeating those lyrics.

Sandy Chapin told Eddie she would send a driver to meet him at the airport and take him to her mansion, where he would stay during the show. When Eddie entered the terminal, he saw a dozen or so men wearing black suits and little chauffeur hats, holding signs with people's names on them. He found one that said *Morrison.*

He walked toward the man carrying the sign. "They call me Eddie Morrison. You looking for me?"

The chauffeur said he was. "Mrs. Chapin sent me. Now, shall we collect your luggage?"

They walked out of the terminal with the baggage, and the chauffeur escorted Eddie over to the biggest, blackest limousine he had ever seen. The driver loaded the luggage in the trunk and opened the door for Eddie. "Please get in, Mr. Morrison."

Eddie couldn't believe what was happening. "I was sitting in the backseat of that limousine being treated like royalty, even though I had holes in the soles of both of my shoes. Man, I felt like I had arrived."

Riding in the back of the limousine and looking at all the people on the streets of New York City, Eddie realized how blessed he was. "I was fascinated. Being from a small town like Tahlequah, I had never seen so many people at one time, and they all seemed to be in a hurry, not at all like the people back home."

When Eddie began his career in art, there was no demand for his work, but now there he was doing a show in New York. He shook his head and said to himself, "I am truly thankful and deeply humbled by my good fortune."

The chauffeur took Eddie to the Chapin mansion in Huntington Park, an affluent village on Long Island, and led him to a guestroom on the third floor. "It was a beautiful mansion with a view of Huntington Bay," Eddie recalled. "Sandy's Adobe Artes Gallery was in her mansion. The show was a big success, as a lot of Sandy's wealthy friends attended and purchased my cedar carvings."

Even after the show, Sandy continued to carry his works in her gallery until she closed it a few years ago.

While there, Eddie decided to take a tour of New York City before returning home. "I was terrified riding on the subway but had a good time while I was there. As I was walking down a crowded street, I saw a hotdog vendor and stood there on the street and ate my hotdog with everything on it, just like in the movies."

When Eddie stepped off the subway in lower Manhattan, he could see the magnificent Twin Towers of the World Trade Center in the distance. He stood in awe as he looked at the 110-story towers, the tallest buildings in the world. "I also visited the Empire State Building and went to the observation deck, where I thought I could see forever. It was a lot of fun."

But when he reflected on the lives of the people of New York City, particularly those in Manhattan, he wondered how they could all live on such a small island. He knew that many of them would never see the rest of the world, and he thought that would be sad.

Following the exhilarating trip to New York and the successful art show in Sandy Chapin's mansion, Eddie went to another show in Phoenix, Arizona. There he entered his relief carving entitled *A Promise for as Long as the Grass Grows* in a juried contest and won a blue ribbon. "Fresh from the Chapin show and this great honor, I was really encouraged and my confidence soared. I was beginning to believe I could be a success if I worked hard and did my best to be faithful to my Cherokee heritage and to the Cherokee people."

One year, the Botanic Gardens in Denver invited Eddie to be the artist in residence during an Allan Houser sculpture exhibit. He enjoyed seeing Houser's artwork again, but Eddie lost one of his tall sculptures during the show. A windstorm blew it over and it broke in two. "It was one of my wild onion pieces." He said losing it really disappointed him, for it was one of his favorites.[2]

Eddie stated that he loves his work and his works and no artist can market that. "You can't explain it, and it's something that unless you feel it, you wouldn't know what I mean."

In April of 2015, the Smithsonian invited Eddie and other Cherokee artists to Washington, D.C., to display their art and give live demonstrations. He said it was an amazing event. "More than 25,000 people visited the museum over the weekend, people from all over the world. There were live art demonstrations, Cherokee storytelling, traditional dance, and melodies of the Cherokee National Youth Choir. Sharing our Cherokee culture and what it means to be Cherokee to our nation's capital was a priceless opportunity. Many of the visitors were so impressed with our presentations, they are planning to visit the Cherokee Nation in Tahlequah to learn more about our people."

Chapter Seven

Family Circle

Eddie's daughter Jennifer Morrison Barker, who lives in Wellington, Kansas, has some wonderful memories of her father. "When I was growing up, we were best buddies and I was a real daddy's girl. Dad taught me to swim when I was four years old. We had an above-the-ground pool and I loved the water. Dad spent a lot of time with me around the pool. He also taught me how to drive. I wasn't even a teenager yet and shouldn't have been driving, but we lived in the country so he would let me drive on the country roads. He also played softball, basketball, and all kinds of games with us."[1]

Jennifer said that sometimes she was a little rebellious as a teen. "But that's what teenagers do. Even though he was firm and always stood by his convictions of what was right and wrong, he was a good dad and I always knew he loved and cared about me."

But she learned early in life that Eddie would not tolerate a bad attitude. "And I learned never to talk back to him."

Some of Jennifer's happiest memories include camping on the Illinois River with her dad and sister, Monica, or swimming in Baron Fork Creek several miles east of Tahlequah. "He taught us to swim and fish using some old cane poles and it was a lot of fun. At night, he would tell us about his childhood and share stories that told us a lot about him."

Eddie's grandmother Jane was always his favorite subject and he spoke of her with great respect and reverence. "He knows and tells others that he would not be where he is today without her help and guidance."

Jennifer was proud of her dad when he became an artist. "I was so excited and knew I was going to have a famous dad. But it didn't happen overnight and took several years for him to become successful. I am thrilled when people honor him and when he receives awards, but I don't think of him as anything other than my dad. Sometimes I forget he is well known across this land and his works are displayed in some of the most famous galleries."

She loves Eddie's art. "He gave me the first piece he ever carved. It is a treasure since it was his first piece. One day I plan to give it to my daughter."

It was the piece Eddie had carved in 1985 out of a piece of wood he found at his grandmother's old house. The wood was from some remnants of a peach tree she had planted in her backyard. He picked up one of the limbs, used his pocketknife to carve the face of an Indian, and gave it to Jennifer.

Some of Eddie's other carvings are also very special to her. "He carved a relief piece for me when I was young. It had cats on it. I have always loved cats so he carved it especially for me. I also have several others."

There was a hint of nostalgia in Jennifer's voice when she talked about her father and the pieces he has given her. "All of them are very close to my heart, for it means I will always have part of my dad with me. And I will always treasure them."

When Jennifer was young, she often went with Eddie to art shows. "I was always proud to see people carefully looking over my dad's work, and it was interesting to see how he dealt with people and made so many friends."

Jennifer believes that when her father was named a Cherokee National Treasure, it was the pinnacle of his success. "I did not get to attend the award ceremony but did go to Tahlequah a few days later for the Cherokee National Holiday. We really celebrated."

Through the years, Jennifer learned that her father has strong personal beliefs. "He is dedicated to everything he loves: his family, his friends, and his art."

As Jennifer has grown older and has had time to reflect on her childhood, she is thankful for all the things she learned from her dad and the good advice he gave to her and her sister, Monica. "He taught us to make the best of every situation and never blame others for our problems. And he cautioned us not to fret over situations beyond our control. He's always had such a wonderful philosophy of life—what's done is done; what will be, will be; and don't give up. Be thankful for all the Creator has blessed us with, and when times are tough, learn from our mistakes and go on."

•••

Eddie's brother Jesse Hummingbird, Jr., is also a distinguished painter with works in the National Museum of the American Indian at the Smithsonian in Washington, D.C. He said he was really proud of Eddie when he decided to pursue a career in art. "I tried to help and mentor him when he was really trying to find his way around in the world of art."[2]

Jesse Hummingbird, a well-known Cherokee Indian artist, was born in Tahlequah, Oklahoma, in 1952. He studied art at Middle Tennessee State University in Murfreesboro. He did further study in life drawing at the American Academy of Art in Chicago. His mediums include pen and ink, prism color, graphite, and acrylic.

Jesse said he and Eddie had been apart for many years but have become a lot closer as they get older. "I try to keep up with him as much as possible. We do about three art shows together each year and we talk on the phone quite a bit."

Jesse lives in Bisbee, Arizona, with his wife, Sandy. Together they have published four children's activity books and produced an animated film for the American Indian Film Institute.

Whenever Jesse and Eddie get together, they share a lot of memories, such as when Eddie started doing his woodcarvings. "He carved out an Indian man, long and slender out of peach wood, and it was very beautiful," said Jesse, recalling one of Eddie's first works. "I bought it from Eddie for five dollars but plan to give it back to him one of these days."

Sometimes Jesse teases Eddie about being so old when he entered art school. "I asked him if they gave him a senior citizens' discount and he just laughed."

Jesse sees a lot of his grandmother Jane in Eddie. "He has a real level head and is slow to anger. He also got Grandma's temperament and I've never seen him mad. She was a wonderful woman and had a profound influence on him. Everyone treated her like she was something special—and she was."

Through the years, the brothers have had some interesting experiences. "On one occasion I helped Eddie deliver a 600-pound sculpture to a lady who lived in Santa Fe. She was one of Eddie's best customers and really praised his work." Her name was Patricia Buffler, a renowned leukemia researcher and faculty member at the University of California at Berkeley. She had a second home in Santa Fe.

Eddie also remembers the large sculpture—a commission piece he carved for the lady. "We had a lot of trouble delivering it because it was so big and heavy."

Moving the 600-pound carving the 700 miles from Eddie's studio in Tahlequah proved to be a difficult task. "Faye's brother Jerry loaded the carving onto the back of my truck with a lift. But after I arrived in Santa Fe, it took my brother Jesse and several others to unload it. I had some friends out there, and Patricia's husband helped us along with some of their neighbors."

They moved the piece slowly down a ramp onto a cart. "But it was so heavy, it smashed the cart into pieces and the sculpture landed on the ground. So we had to find a bigger, stronger cart and then all of us together were able to lift the piece up on the cart and move it to the backyard, where we unloaded it."

•••

Monica Morrison Glass, who lives in Broken Arrow, Oklahoma, is also proud of her father's work and his success. "It's awesome to know of his early days and how he has overcome so many things on his road to success. His work is a testimony to his life."[3]

Like her sister, Jennifer, Monica has a lot of memories of her dad—some of them not so happy. "Once when I was sixteen, my dad and I were sitting on the tailgate of his pickup while he was carving a little piece of wood with his pocketknife. Suddenly he dropped the piece of wood and looked at me and said, 'Monica, just stay calm but I need you to take me to the hospital to the emergency room.'"

At first she didn't know what he was talking about, but then she saw blood all over his hand. "He had cut off his finger."

Scared and trembling, she drove him to the hospital. "And the doctors sewed his finger back on."

Monica was always fascinated as she watched Eddie work in his studio. "His works are just beautiful but, of course, I'm a little biased."

Sometimes she sees her dad on television or hears people raving about his work and she shouts, "Yeah, that's my dad!"

Monica always enjoyed going with Eddie to his art shows. "Even when I was only a little girl and maybe six years old, going with my dad was so special and it was fun seeing all the other artists and their paintings or carvings."

Eddie didn't have a lot of money during the early days, so they slept in the back of his pickup truck with the camper shell on it. Monica recalls the bad storm that he had also talked about. "The pickup was shaking and I was really scared. But after awhile, the storm passed and we went back to sleep."

One of her favorite memories is when he would buy her things at the art shows. "Sometimes he would buy me something like a little piece of turquoise jewelry. That meant a lot to me when I was a little girl."

Although Monica also was unable to attend the Cherokee National Treasure ceremony, she was so proud of her father when she learned of the award. "He is so deserving, for he has spent his entire life determined to make something good out of his days of small beginnings. God is so amazing to choose my dad's life and turn it into a testimony to others that says no matter how impossible things seemed in the beginning, God blessed him double and beyond for all the setbacks and trials he had to face. I know in my heart that dad deserved the award and I am so happy for him. I thought back to what he had told me about the early years and I realized how far he has come. How he started out with just a pocketknife and a little piece of wood. My goodness—from sleeping in the back of his old truck to being named Cherokee National Treasure! How great is that? Yeah, I'm really proud of him."

When Monica learns that Eddie is to appear on television in the Tulsa area, she gets so excited and can't wait for the program to begin. "I call my friends and tell them about it and always post it on Facebook, for I am so proud."

Chapter Eight

Passing the Torch

Eddie has a passion to help young Cherokees become successful artists so they, too, can keep their native culture alive for future generations.

There are at least two prerequisites to success in the world of art, and Eddie knows them well. "I am confident that if a young artist loves what he is doing, he will do whatever it takes to succeed. He must also have what I call 'staying power,' or determination."

Through the years, Eddie has seen a number of young artists who had great abilities but failed. "They just couldn't stay with it. Some of them gave up because they lost their vision and passion or perhaps because of financial disappointment. Just fell by the wayside."

When he talks about the young artists, one senses he really cares about them and would do anything he can to help them become successful. However, he said with a half-smile, half-frown, "I always try to warn them that if they want to be successful, they should be prepared to take a vow of poverty—especially in the early years."

Eddie would like to wave a magic wand and grant the young artists instant success, but he knows it doesn't work like that. "I want to raise the standard for the young artists and do everything I can to empower them to greatness. But I have to be honest with them and explain they must have a lot of self-discipline and toughness to make it in the Native American world of art."[1]

Eddie has learned many important life lessons through the years, and he wants to pass them on to the younger men and women. "I hope I can use my gift to inspire some young artist who is having a tough time and tell him, 'You can make it. You can become successful. Just fasten your tool belt, pick up your hammer and chisel, and keep going.'"[2]

Eddie is there for the young artists and ready to lend a helping hand. "There was one young Cherokee who didn't have any tools, so I gave him some of my old ones. Recently he came up to me at an art show and thanked me for the tools I had given him and said he was using them."

Successful artists such as Eddie must be very careful how they deal with young artists who come to them to show them their work. Although he knows he must always be truthful, he tries to be gentle in his critique. "I know that a young artist can be destroyed by just a few critical words."

He knows what it's like, for there have been times when he has had his feelings hurt by others, and some of them surprised him. "I've tried to donate some of my art to the museum at my alma mater, the Institute, in Santa Fe. Even though when I graduated the faculty named me the outstanding student in the three-dimensional art department, museum officials turned down my offer. They said it was not contemporary enough. And that's very interesting, for I have had other art collectors tell me my work is not traditional enough."

Today Eddie specializes in three-dimensional art rendered in wood, stone, and bronze. Some of the pieces detail curvy-shaped bears or the faces of Cherokees caped in bear's fur. He calls his work "contemporary traditional" and thinks perhaps that will satisfy everyone.[3]

Through the years, various schools have invited Eddie to speak to their art students and give demonstrations. At first, his old fear of speaking before groups came back to haunt him. "So during some of the demonstrations, I solved my problem and told the students to watch me work, and then I would start carving a piece of cedar or chipping away at a block of stone and that seemed to work out okay."

On one occasion, a school in Kansas asked him to appear in a video they were producing, which would show him demonstrating his carving technique to the gifted children in their art department. He had never been in a video before and wondered if he would be nervous. At first it was a little difficult trying to teach with the cameras following every move he made. "These were gifted, art-oriented students. I told them, 'The best thing I can do is show you how to do it. So watch me carefully.' Then I took a piece of limestone and carved it right there in front of them. It was quite a show. I was chipping away with a hand chisel, the students were watching with rapt attention, chips were flying everywhere, and the cameras were rolling."[4]

Apparently the video was a huge success. "The students were fascinated with the presentation and asked a lot of questions, such as how I decide what image to carve, how long did it take to develop the skills, and, of course, what does it take to become an artist. And it was all caught on film, which really turned out good."

After long years in the profession—enduring the good times and the bad—Eddie has come to the conclusion that art students must open their minds to all the possibilities of an artist's career. "Young artists

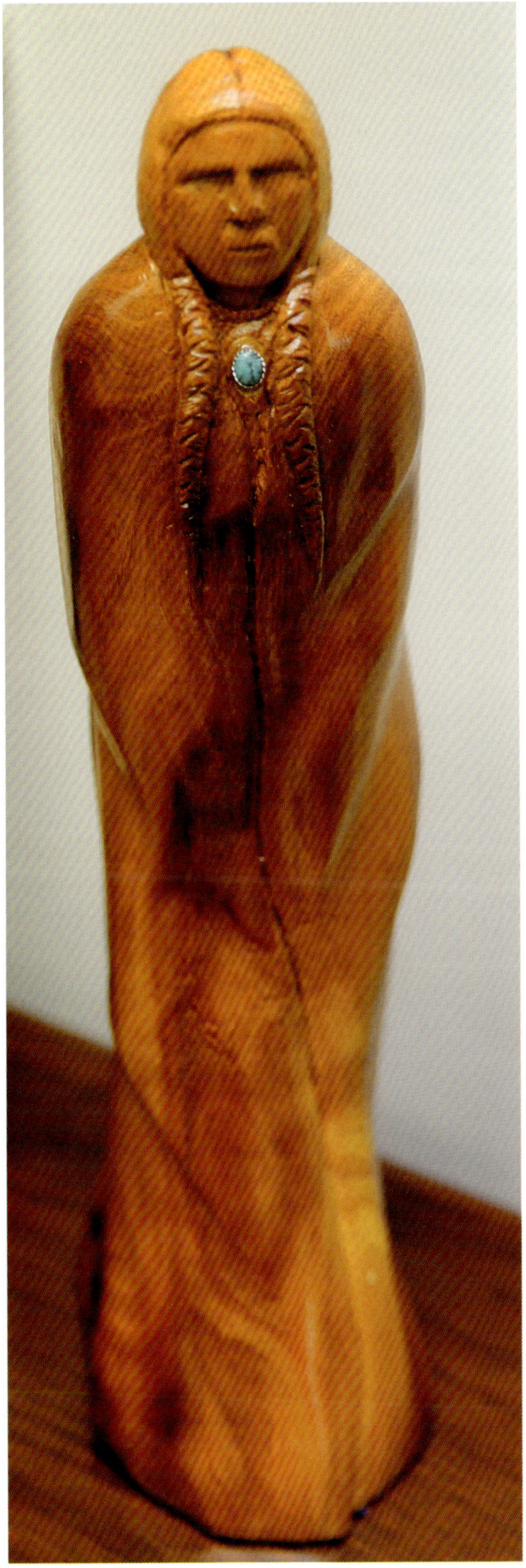

Robed Cherokee maiden with turquoise

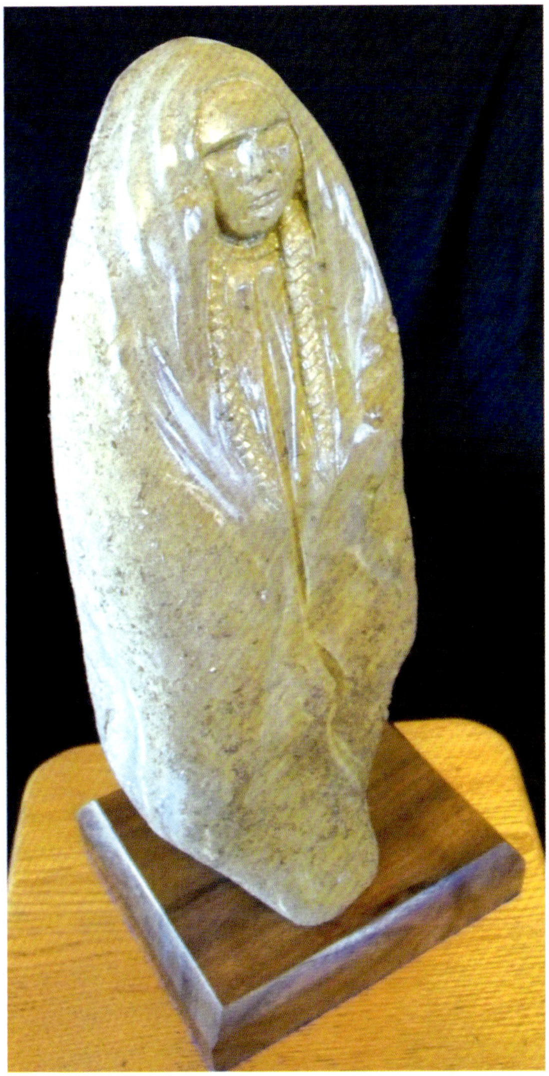

Native American woman with braids, carved from limestone (Photograph by Brandon Scott)

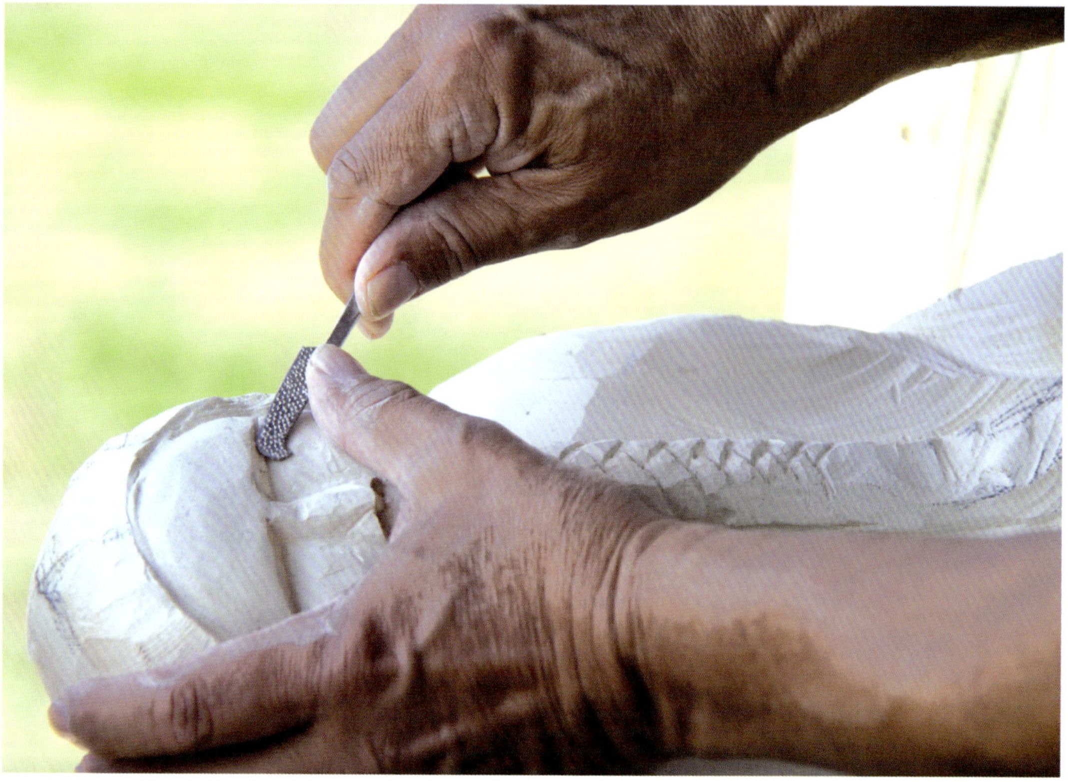

Eddie carving facial details in a piece of limestone

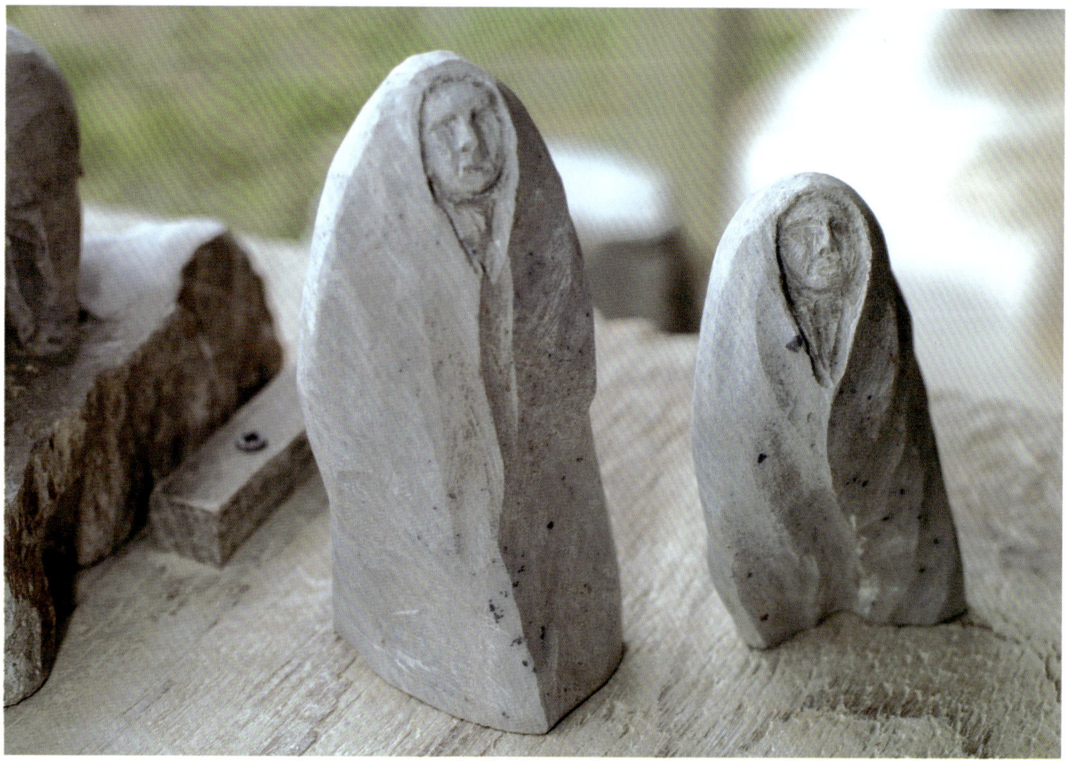

Steatite pieces in progress

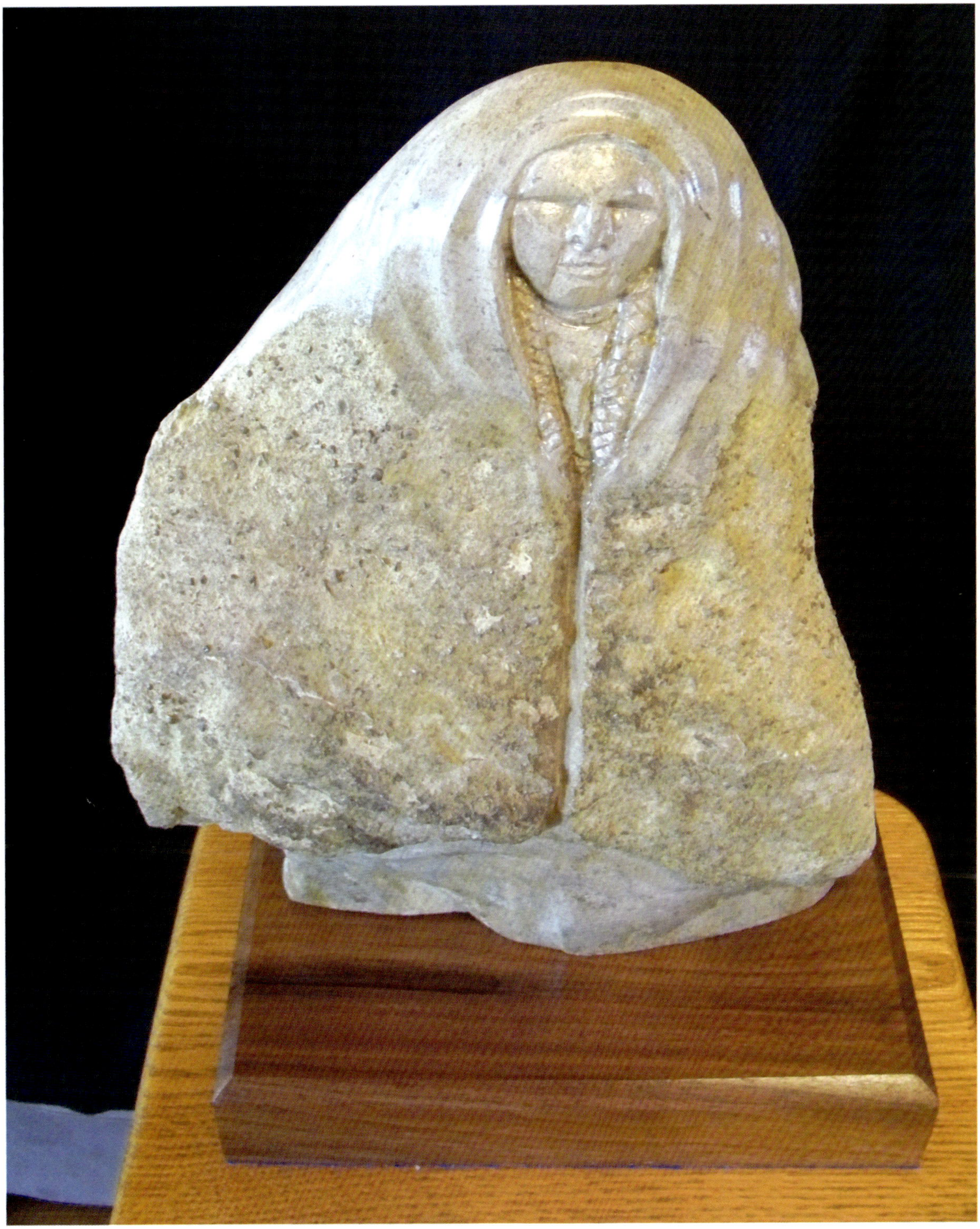

Robed figure carved from limestone

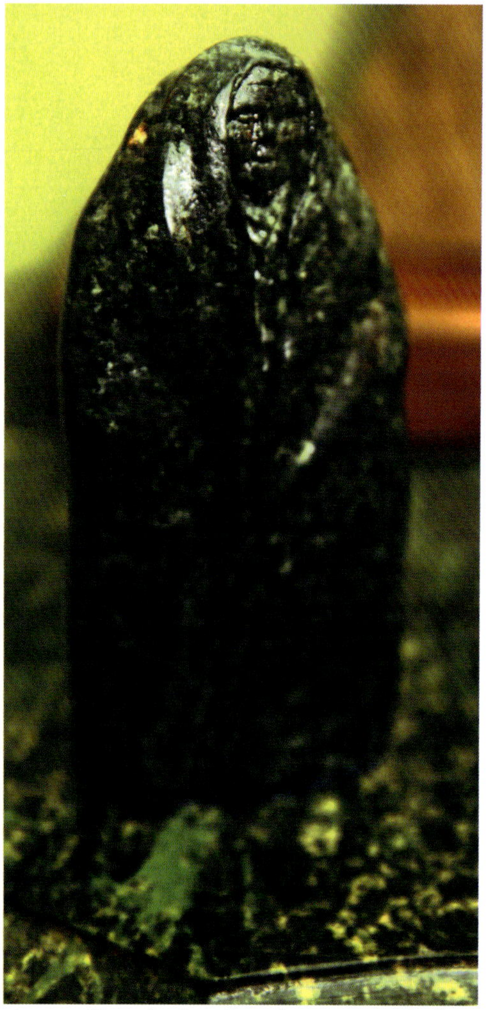

A small robed Cherokee, carved from steatite (Photograph by Brandon Scott)

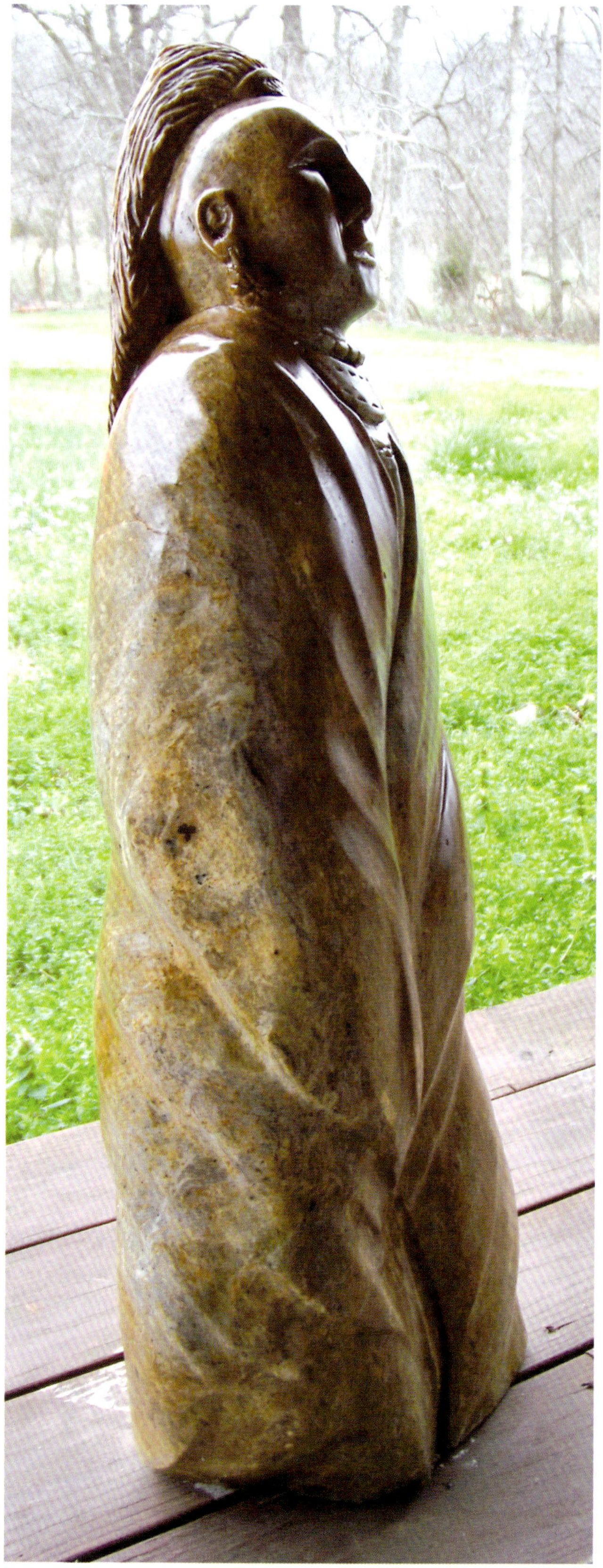

A polished steatite carving of a Native American with a topknot

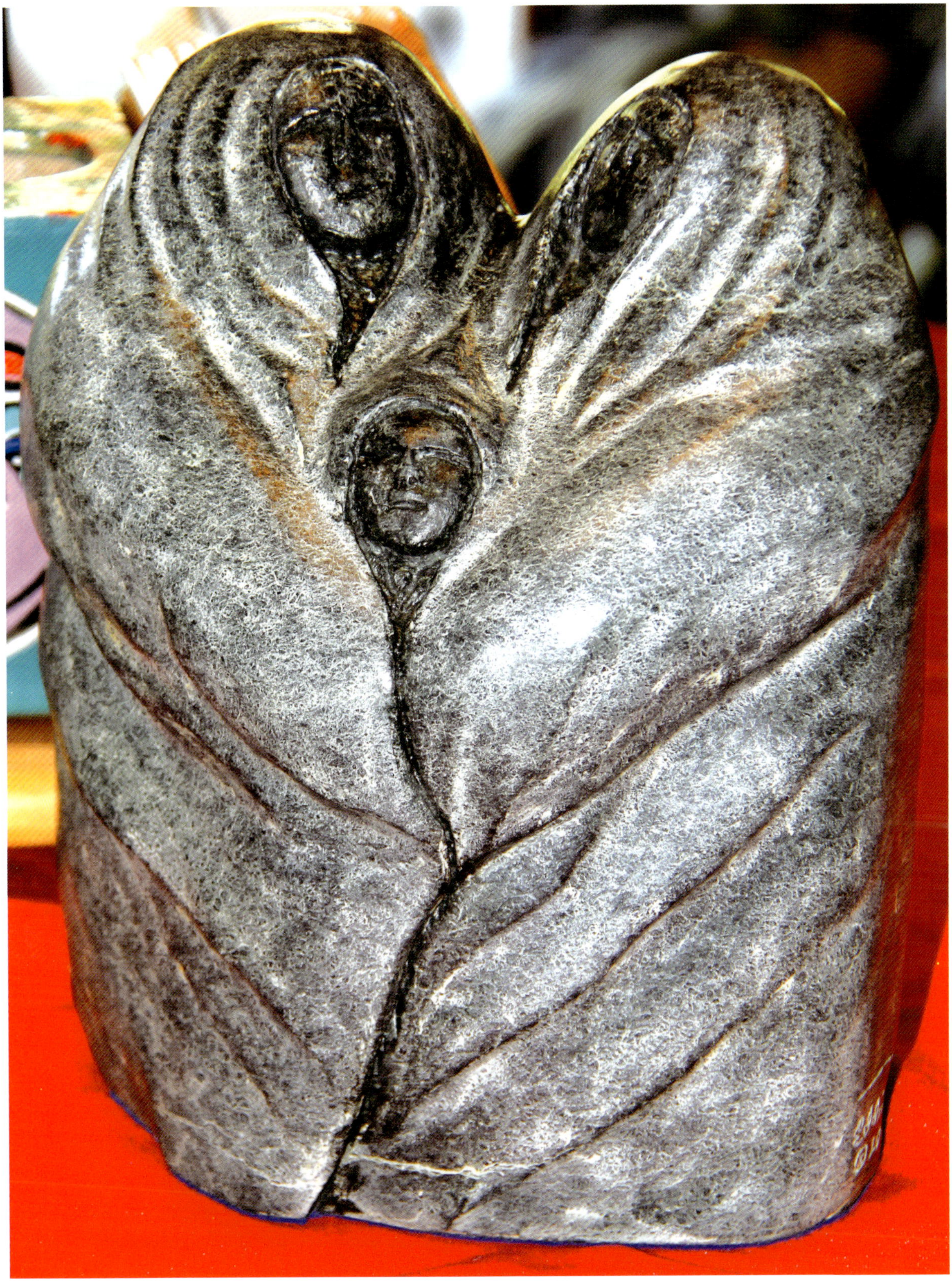

A Native American family wrapped in a blanket, carved from steatite (Photograph by Jamie Murphy, *Cherokee Phoenix*)

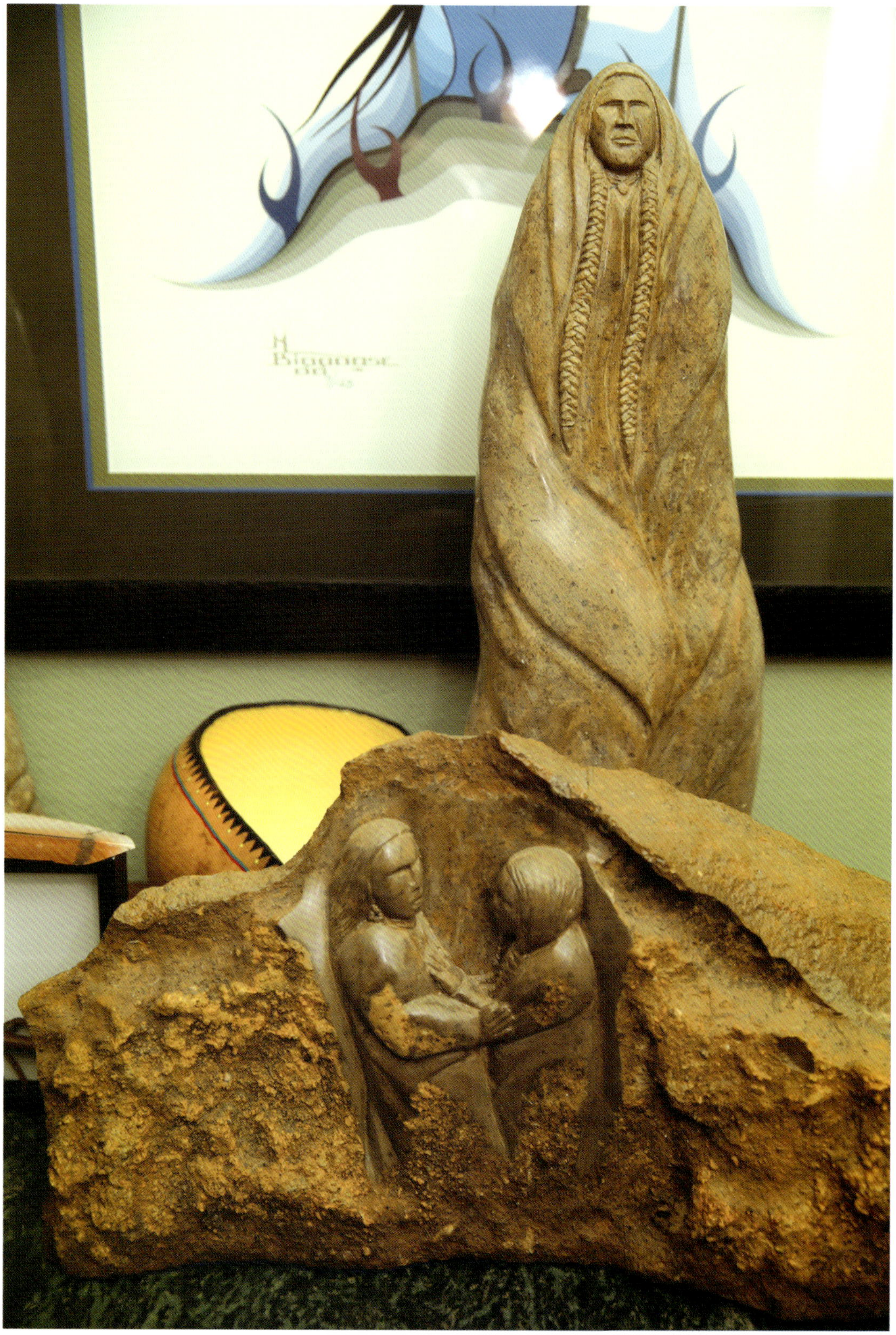

Stone carving of a Cherokee woman with children

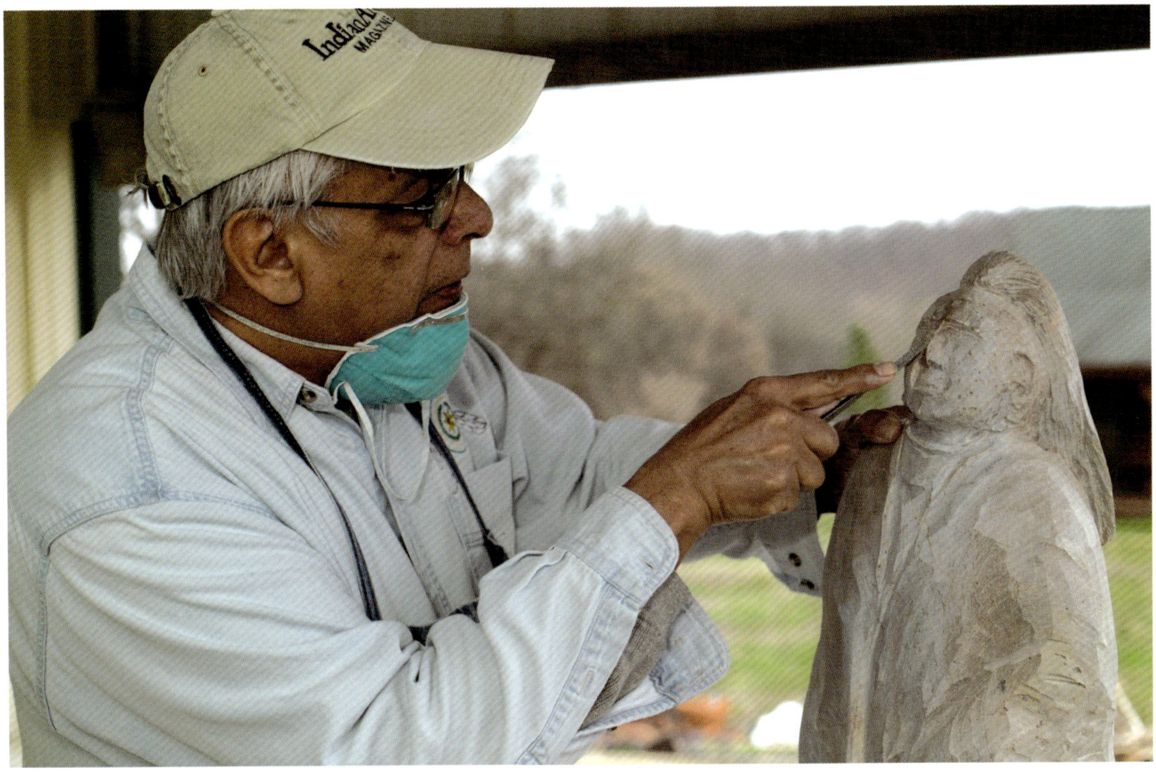

Eddie carving a Cherokee warrior in steatite

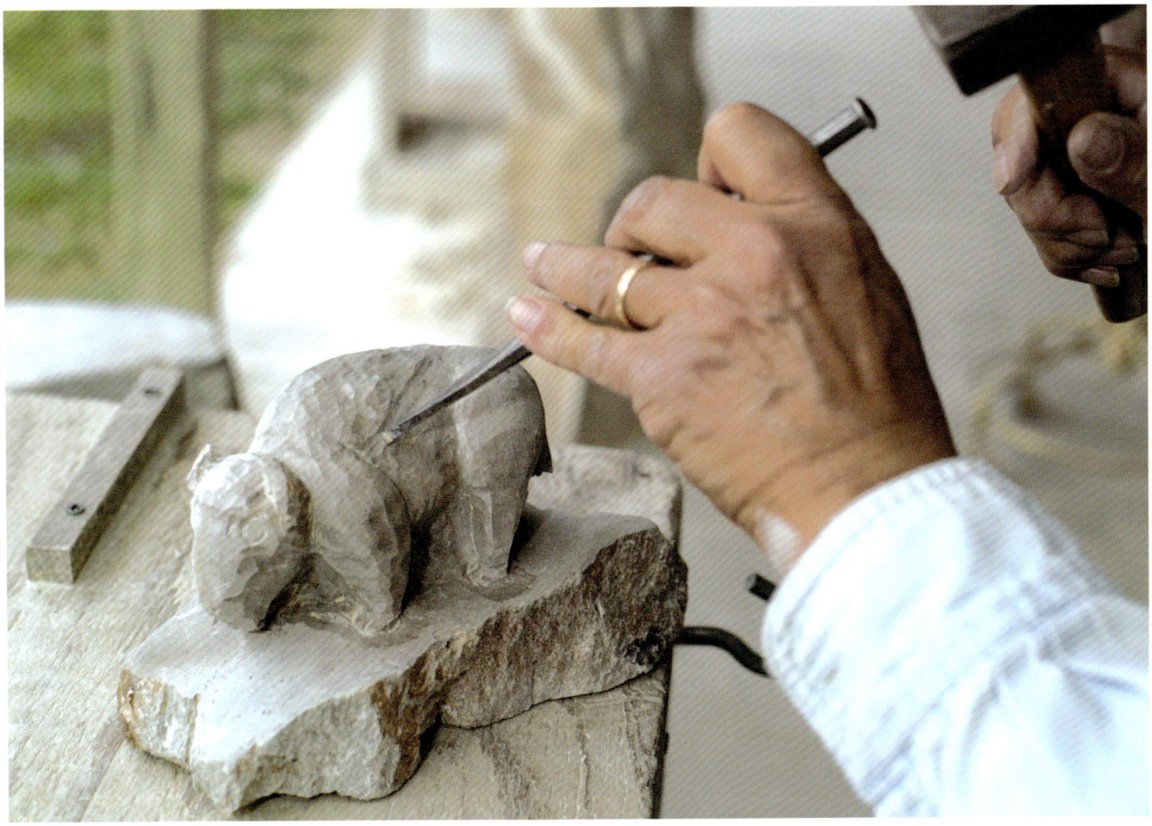

Eddie detailing a steatite carving of a buffalo (Photograph by Brandon Scott)

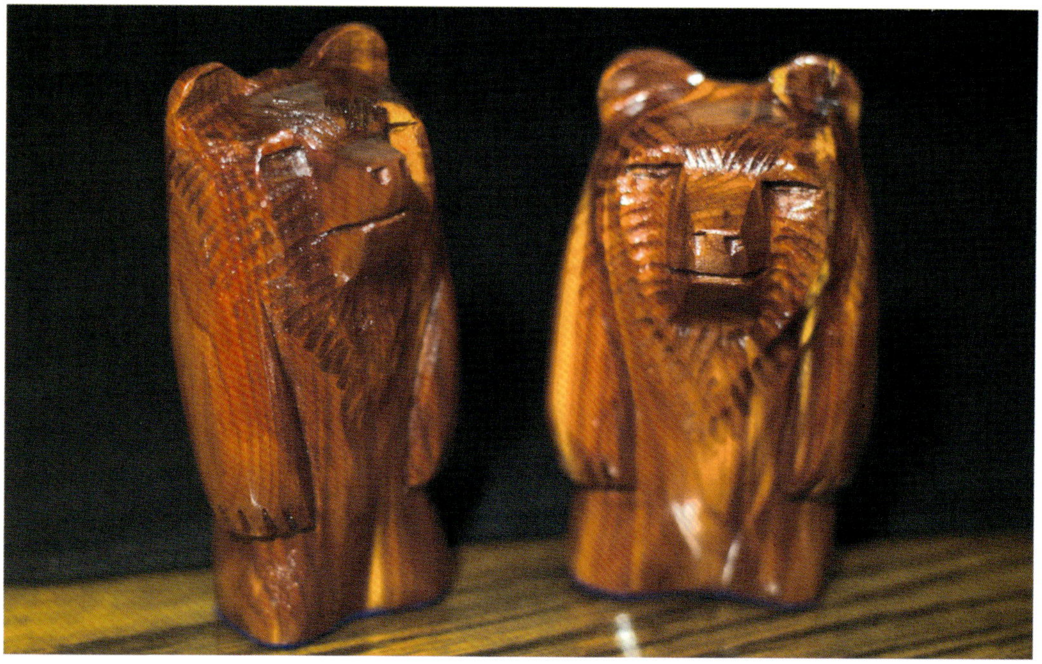

Two small bears carved from cedar (Photograph by Brandon Scott)

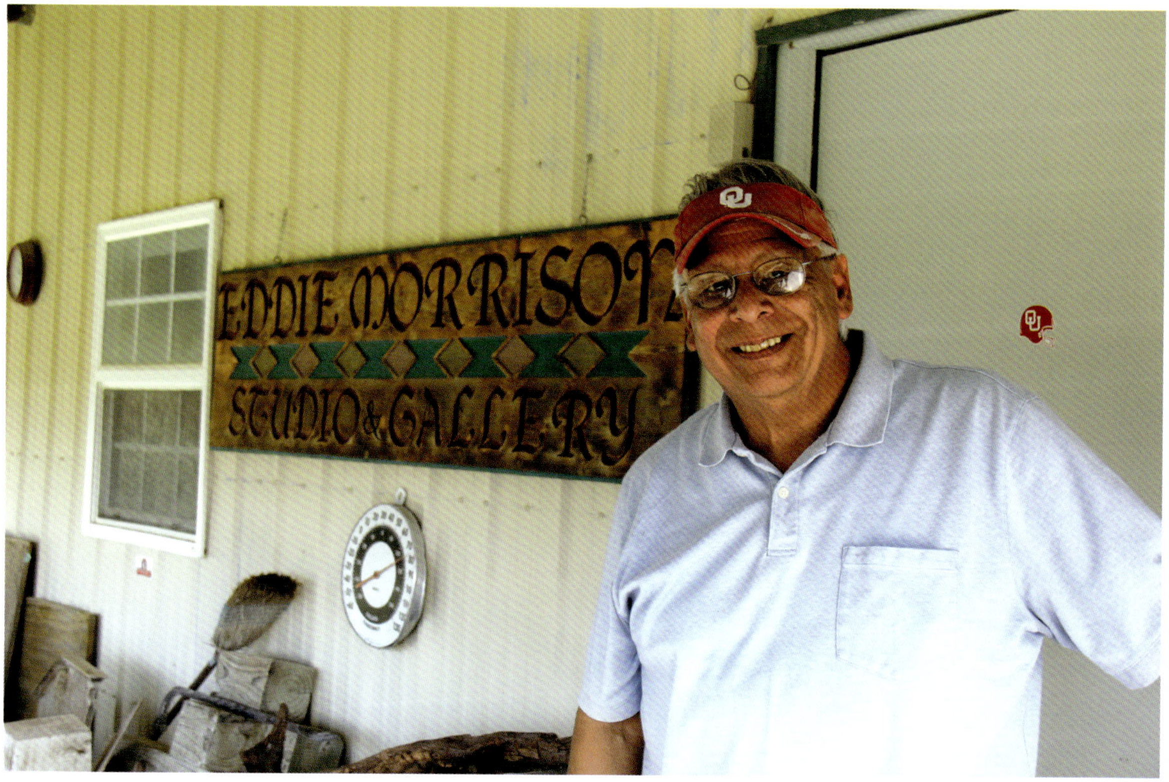

Eddie standing in front of his studio on Steely Hollow Road (Photograph by Jamie Murphy, *Cherokee Phoenix*)

may think, 'I can draw a face but I can't cut a stone.' I tell them, 'You can't learn to successfully cut a stone until you have done it a thousand times. If you really want to do it, you will keep trying, and one day you will see the picture that was born in your mind unveiled in the stone right before your eyes.' But don't give up! And don't expect your first piece to be a masterpiece unless you are exceptionally gifted. And don't expect to start making a lot of money, as that will take a long, long time."

Unfortunately, some young artists think it's going to be easy and buyers for galleries will be knocking on their doors wanting to purchase their work. "But it's a long and lonely road that leads to success, and these young people must do whatever it takes and believe they are winners and not losers. If they do that, they will succeed."

When Eddie remembers the early days, he admits there were times when he, too, was disappointed with his life's work. "Oh, I think a lot of times you kind of get down, because you don't have any money and you're struggling and you think nobody likes your work and sometimes because you can go to shows and not sell a thing. I've learned over the years to just go on down the road to the next show."[5]

Eddie dreams of an eternal twilight for Cherokee young people in general and young artists in particular.

After they get acquainted with him, young artists understand that he knows what he's talking about and listen to his advice. They are always amazed when they learn he has created thousands of works of art through the years and one year did more than two hundred.

Deep in his heart, Eddie believes that the best advice he could give to any young artist is this: "Right now you may not fully realize how difficult it is to become a successful artist. But if you have a passion for art in your heart, it will never go away. You can do whatever you dream."[6]

There has been a revival of interest in Cherokee art and artists, and Eddie attributes a lot of it to Chief Baker. He says the chief really has a passion to promote Cherokee artists so that Cherokee people will never forget their culture, history, and traditions.

Chapter Nine

Tributes

Today people throughout the land know Eddie as an artist and also as a man with a great passion to create works of art that represent Cherokee people with dignity and pride. Many of his friends in the world of art recognize his unique talents and have good things to say about him.

Susan Pourian, director of the Indian Craft Shop in the Department of the Interior in Washington, D.C., greatly admires his work. "His art is very unique. Eddie has really captured a few different figures—the bear in cedar and limestone and caped figures in wood. Our customers really love them."[1]

Since 1938, the Indian Craft Shop has represented artists from forty-five Indian tribes throughout the nation. It has the reputation of displaying authentic Native American art, and people from all over the world visit the shop to admire and purchase the works.

Pourian had other praise for Eddie. "Eddie Morrison has devoted his lifetime to art working with the natural mediums of wood and stone and has represented the Cherokee Nation with great honor to the world. He has generated exposure and interest in the life, ways, and culture of the Cherokee and he bridges the past to the present. His work is based on traditions and history with permanent creations of spirit and beauty in today's contemporary world.

"Through consistent and active participation in juried art shows across the nation, Eddie has remained a devoted representative of the Cherokee and of the American Indian peoples. Working to honor life and natural elements, Eddie's sculpture brings out the beauty of natural materials and captures a moment in time of life that generates thought and insight. He is well respected among his peers, galleries, and clients and is humble in his accomplishments."

Pourian recalled that in 2001, the shop was asked to set up a display of Indian art to welcome Gale Norton, the incoming U.S. secretary of the

Interior. Fifteen items were selected. "One of those was Eddie's medium-sized cedar carving of an eagle. Each piece of art had a tent placard recognizing the materials, name of the artist, and the tribe represented."

Pourian stated that a year later, all items from the display—except Eddie's eagle carving—were removed to make room for other Indian works of art. "Eddie's eagle carving remained on display until Secretary Norton's service ended in 2006."

She pointed out, "Eddie's sculptures bring out the beauty of the natural materials and capture a moment in time allowing him to share his own story and that of his tradition."

According to Pourian, two of his limestone pieces were also placed in the Interior Department's patio garden.

•••

At the Cherokee Arts Center in Tahlequah, Indian artists meet, share their knowledge, and learn new artistic techniques. They also show and sell their work. Donna Tinnin, the director of the center's Spider Gallery, said Eddie is one of the most pleasant and likeable people she has ever met. "And for his art, we can't seem to keep it in the gallery for it sells so quickly."[2]

On one occasion, Tinnin called Eddie and told him she needed some more pieces of his art because the gallery had sold out. "He told me his inventory was depleted so I told him, 'You better get to crackin'.' Now that is our saying when we meet up with one another, 'You better get to crackin'."

•••

Callie Chunestudy, with the Spider Gallery, also has some good things to say about Eddie and his work. She believes that people are attracted to its deep sense of culture and tradition. "He can evoke the strongest emotion in the simplest details."[3]

Chunestudy added that his work is never "busy or crowded." "I really enjoy the way he leaves natural parts of the stone or wood exposed. His execution leaves a warmth in his pieces that is rarely achieved in stone carving."

She always enjoys visiting with Eddie when he comes to the gallery to deliver one of his works of art for display. "He has an easy way about him and a fabulous sense of humor. I have not met another artist that does not admire his work. I believe it is held as a standard to which other works are compared."

•••

Jane Osti of Tahlequah—also a well-known artist—has high praise for Eddie's art. Her respect centers around how he connects with his work. "It's how he feels about the wood and the stone. He has a respect for the sacredness of Nature."[4]

She believes there is an unusual spiritual depth in his work. "That's the feeling I get when I'm around him and from his work. He is also a very humble person—sometimes ornery but humble. We've been joking around with each other for twenty-five years."

As contemporaries, she and Eddie often attended the same art shows, especially in the early days of their careers. She has a lot of memories, some of them quite interesting. "We've known each other through the good times and the bad, the highs and the lows. Some of the shows we attended were very successful—others were not. But we both paid our dues traveling across the country trying to get to the shows."

She remembers once when she rode in the back of Eddie's pickup to a show in Arizona. "We were on our way to Phoenix from Oklahoma, over 1,100 miles. But he had a camper shell in the back of the truck to keep the rain out."

The Cherokee Nation has named Jane a Cherokee National Treasure for her beautiful pottery works.

•••

Victoria Vasquez, a Cherokee Tribal Councilor, says Eddie's artwork is renowned all across the United States and his sculptures are exhibited and sold at some of the most prestigious art galleries in the country, including the Smithsonian. She has always admired Eddie's work and believes he is an outstanding artist. "He is an exceptional sculptor and award-winning, accomplished artist. I have known him for many years. He continually sets himself apart from others in the art world by exhibiting professional behavior, strong beliefs and high moral character. Eddie's good heart and sense of humor endear him to many."[5]

Vasquez, a recipient of the Cherokee National Treasure Master Craftsman award for her beautiful Southeastern woodlands-style pottery, says Eddie has an engaging sense of humor. "That's one of the things I love most about him. It seems in the Indian community, artist or not, humor plays a big role in our lives."

•••

Perhaps the greatest tribute to Eddie's work was when the Smithsonian National Museum of the American Indian in Washington, D.C., invited him to participate in Cherokee Days in April 2015. The invitation read, in part, "As a Cherokee National Treasure you will have an opportunity to meet with thousands of visitors and showcase your talents as well as the culture of the Cherokee people. As part of this event you will be able to show, sell and demonstrate your work."

Cherokee Chief Baker is proud of Eddie and the other Cherokee artists who participated in Cherokee Days at the Smithsonian. Before the event, he stated, "Preserving our culture means sharing it with the next generation, and that's what we will be doing as we showcase our talented artisans and highly respected historians at the Smithsonian Institute."

•••

In 2001, the Cherokee Heritage Center honored Eddie by choosing his *Strength of Life* design for the Cherokee Nation's official Christmas ornament. According to a spokesman for the center, "One side of this ornament has the Cherokee 'seven-point star' around the circle of life, which has the four directions in the center. The symbol is found in ancient mound builders' designs and is used in ancient Cherokee stories. The other side has a star, which symbolizes the One for whom Christmas is celebrated. This ornament, all together, represents 'strength of life.'"

The Cherokee Heritage Center, located in the Cherokee Nation in Tahlequah, is the cultural center for Cherokee tribal history, culture, and the arts. It offers educational programs, reconstructed historic villages, exhibits, and scholarly research. At the Cherokee Family Research Center, Cherokee descendents can reconnect with their ancestors. The Cherokee Heritage Center also houses historic tribal documents and artifacts dating back to the 1700s.

•••

In 2014, during the ninth annual Cherokee Art Market, *Tulsa Voice* magazine wrote a tribute to Eddie: "Eddie Morrison's sculptures look like they climbed right out of the earth. They share a likeness with the work of iconic native sculptor Allan Houser."[6]

The magazine article also noted that early in Eddie's career, Houser was his mentor. "Native pride and dignity is a common thread through the work of both Morrison and Houser, but Houser encouraged Morrison to find his own style."

Tulsa Voice noted that the late sculptor's influence on Eddie transcends their craft and reminded its readers that he often pays tribute to the master craftsman, Houser.

•••

Eddie considers it a special honor when his friends purchase and enjoy his art. Such a friend is Buddy McCarty, a successful insurance agent in Owasso, Oklahoma. Although Eddie never met him at Northeastern, he and Buddy attended the university at the same time.[7]

Years later, they met at an art show in Tulsa and became best friends. But more than that, Buddy was fascinated with Eddie's work and became his greatest supporter. Through the years, he has purchased more than twenty pieces of Eddie's art. He displays them in his home, insurance office, and even a log cabin out in the country near Locust Grove, Oklahoma.

Buddy is proud of his friend Eddie's work. "One of my favorites is *Wild Onions,* which shows an Indian woman holding a bundle of wild onions. I tell everyone that my friend Eddie Morrison carved it and that's what makes it so special."

Anyone who is around Buddy for any length of time will hear him talk about his friend Eddie. "He is a great person and wonderful man. He is very proud of being Cherokee, as am I."

Buddy said one of Eddie's sculptures is particularly special to him. "Eddie found a large rock in his sister's backyard and turned it into the sculpture of an Indian warrior. It's the heaviest piece I own."

During the Cherokee National Holiday, Buddy invited Eddie to go with him for a cornstalk shoot at the Sequoyah Training School, south of Tahlequah. "Eddie said he couldn't go because he didn't have a bow. So I told him I would loan him a new one I had just purchased."

However, things didn't go exactly as Buddy had planned. "Eddie broke my new bow! Since then some of the other cornstalk shooters call him 'Broken Bow.'"

Their friendship has lasted through the years. They get together from time to time and always enjoy talking about Buddy's favorite subject—Eddie's art.

•••

Dr. Isabel Baker, his high-school speech teacher, said that although

Eddie is a renowned artist, he is still the same old Eddie whom his friends have loved and admired. "He has a quiet, humble spirit about him."[8]

Following his career for many years, she has been pleased to see him faithful to the Cherokee people and, with his wife, Faye, always helping others. "Whether it is a hog fry, gospel singing, or fund-raising dinner for a good cause, you can count on them to be there. He travels all over America from Washington, D.C. to many other states and, as he travels, he takes time to help many other artists fulfill their dreams. He is a highly respected artist with great natural ability, but also a man who dearly loves his family and friends and the Cherokee people."

•••

Julie Pearson-Little Thunder interviewed Eddie and said, "At first glance, Eddie Morrison's sculpture appears simple and unassuming but, as the artist points out, creating that impression requires time-intensive labor."

Although Eddie is proud of all the compliments he has received from his friends and the managers and owners of art galleries, he says the greatest tribute he could ever receive is when someone purchases one of his wood or stone carvings and takes it home with them to enjoy both today and far into the future. "But the ultimate compliment I ever received was when a blind woman ran her hand over the face of one of my sculptures, caressed it with her fingers, and said, 'That's beautiful.'"

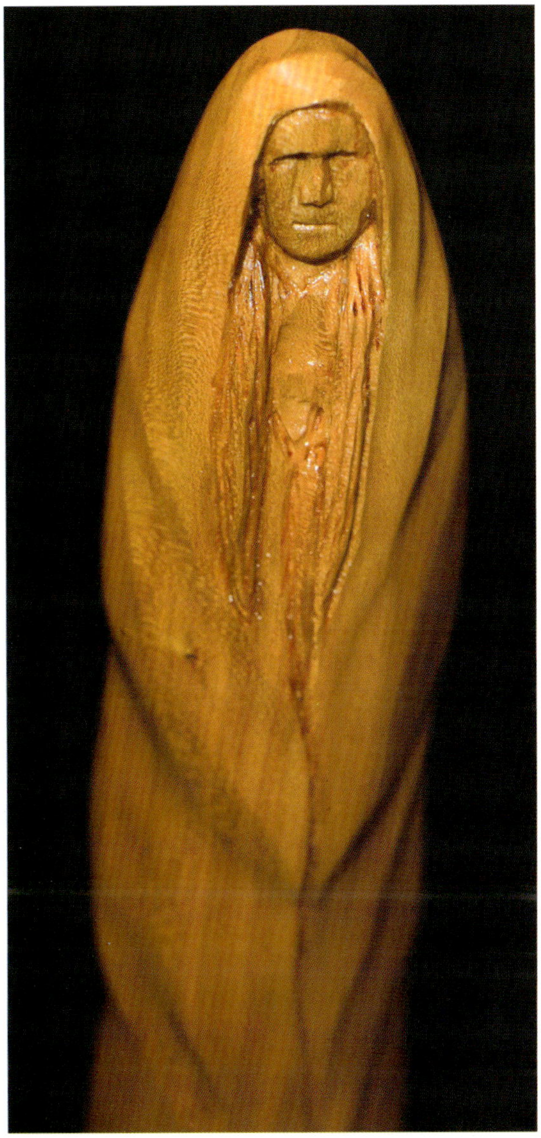

Robed Native American (Photograph by Brandon Scott)

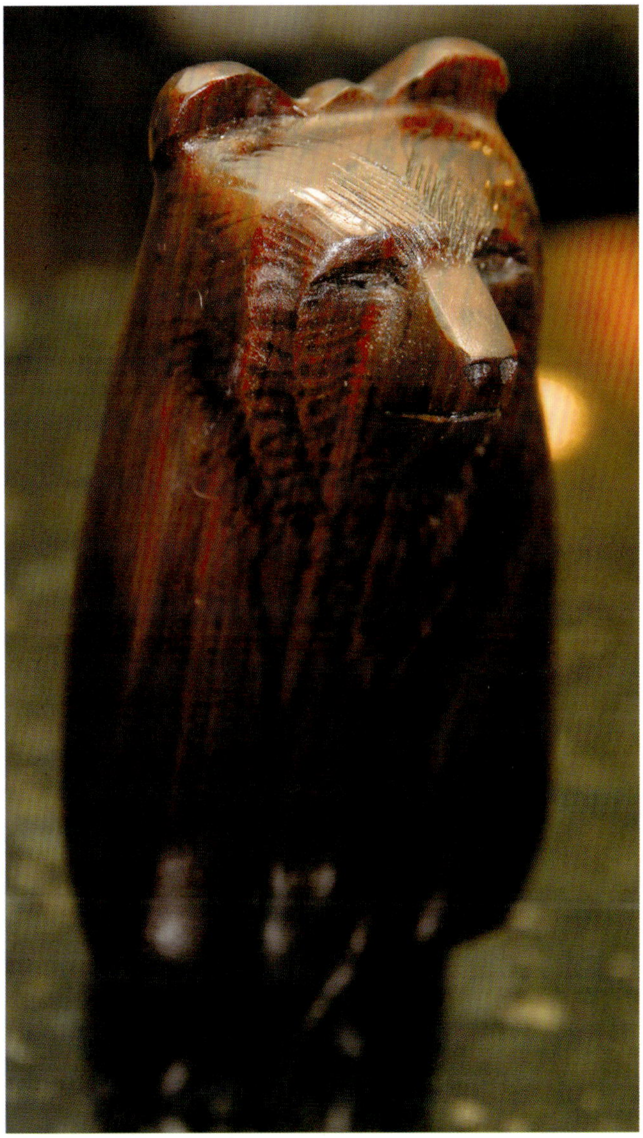

Bear carved from black walnut (Photograph by Brandon Scott)

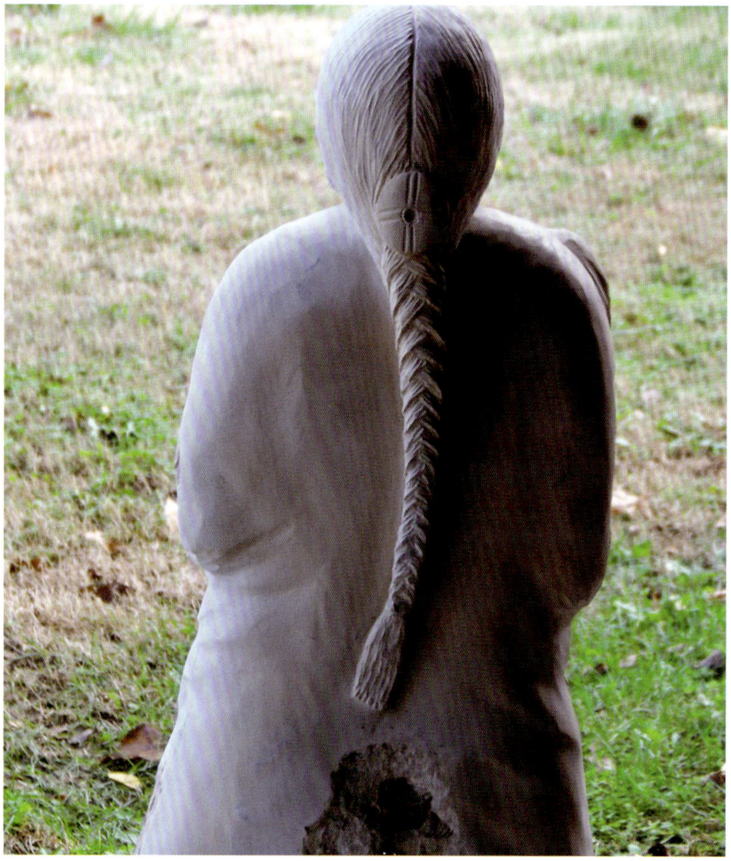

Indian maiden's braid, carved from Kansas limestone

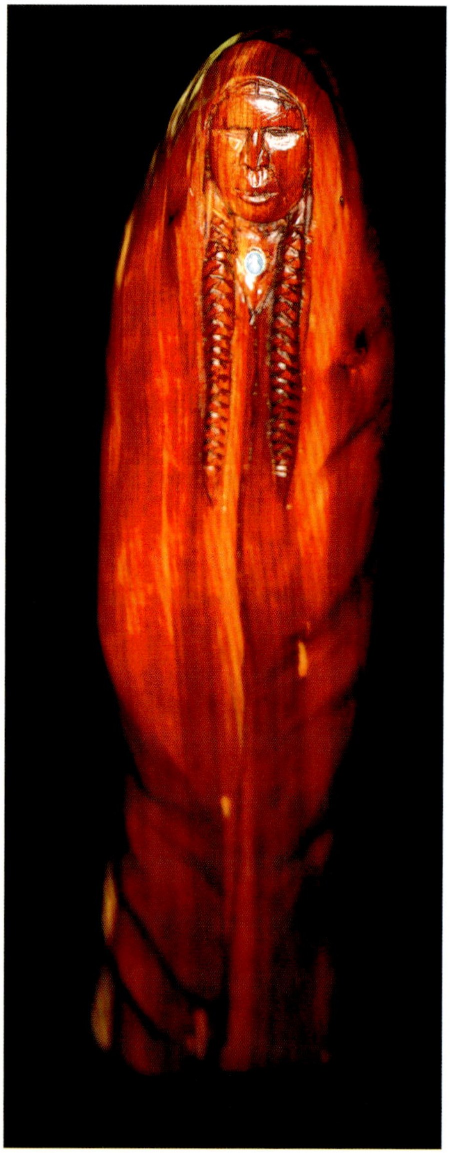

Robed Native American wearing turquoise, carved from cedar

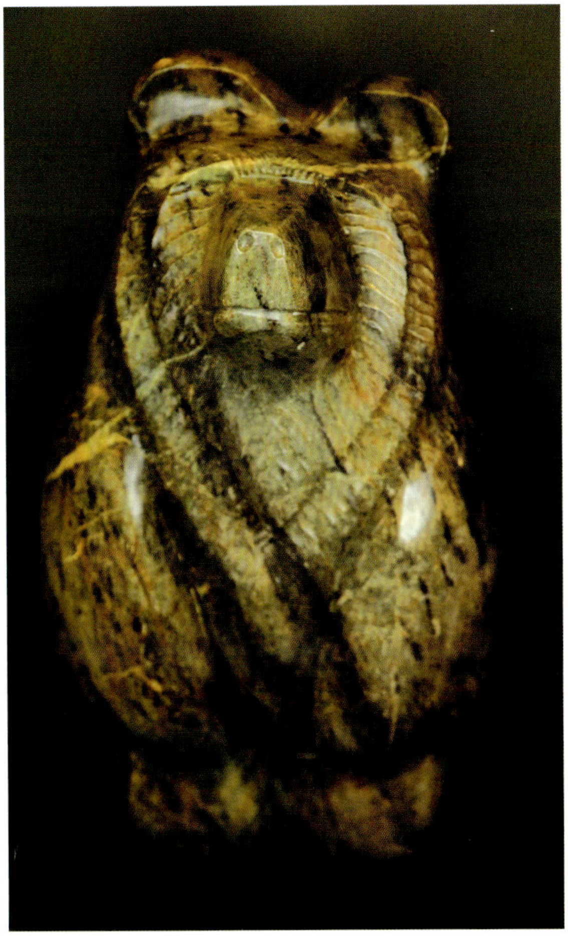

Bear carved from British Columbia steatite (Photograph by Brandon Scott)

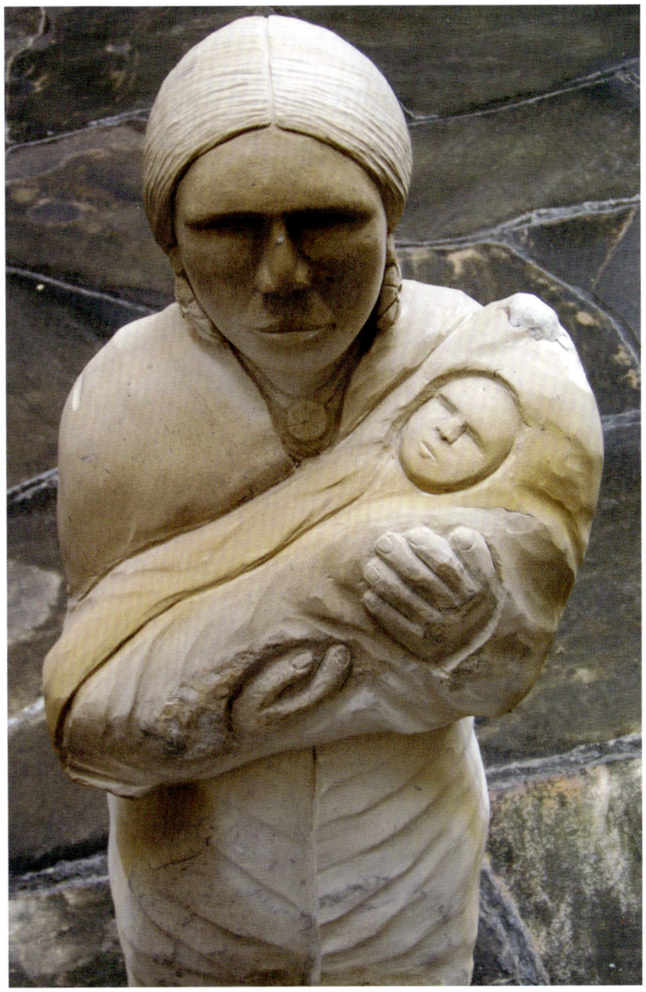

Mother and Child, *located in the garden of the Department of the Interior, Washington, D.C.*

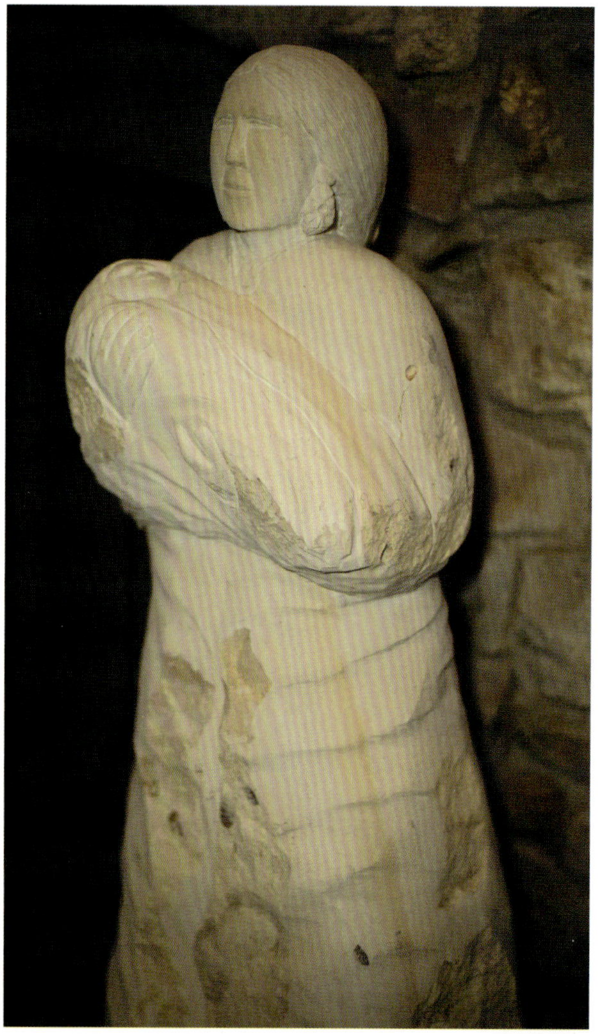

Limestone carving of a mother and child (Photograph by Brandon Scott)

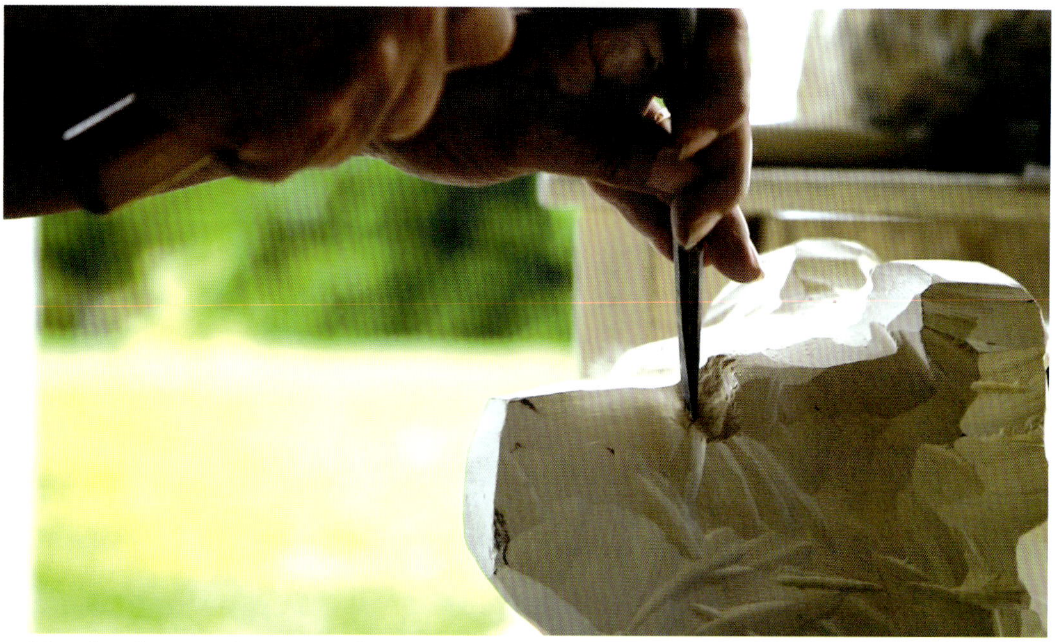

Eddie chisels out a bear's eye from limestone (From *A Man's Legend*, www.TribalTV.org, produced and directed by Celia Xavier, IndieIn Films © 2015)

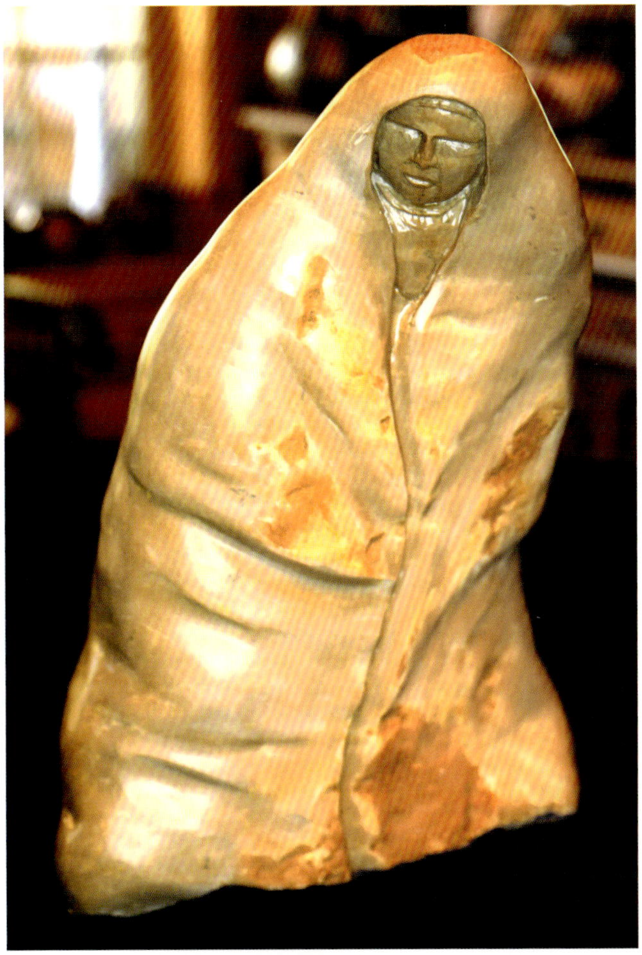

Robed Native American woman

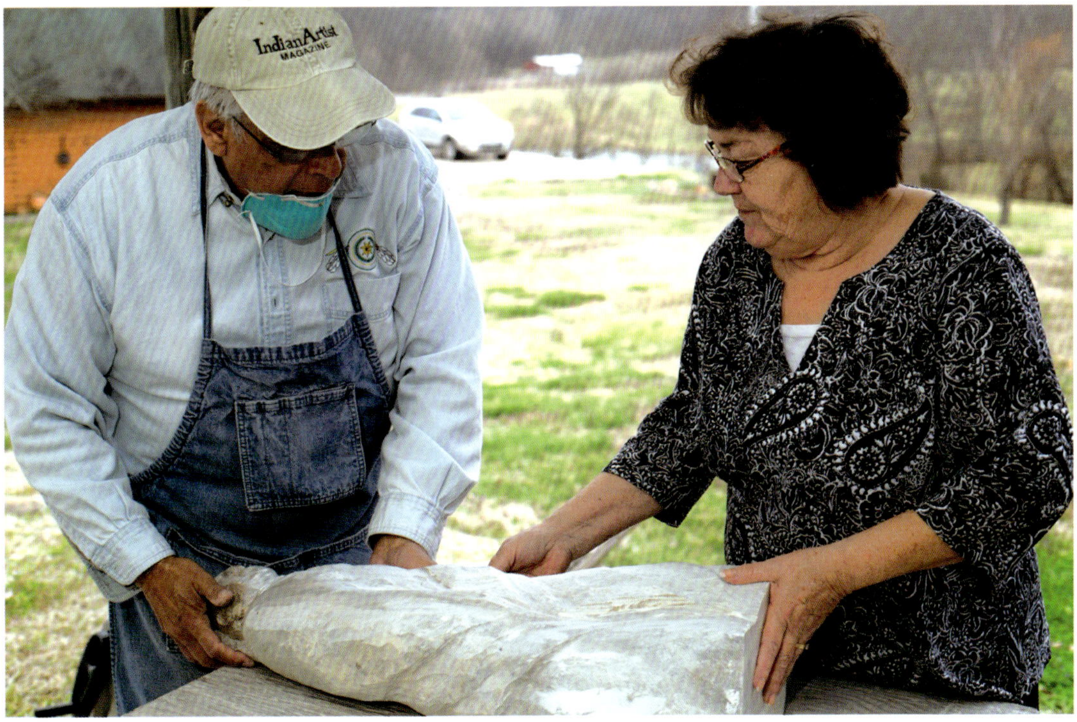

Eddie and his wife, Faye, lifting a large piece of stone (Photograph by Brandon Scott)

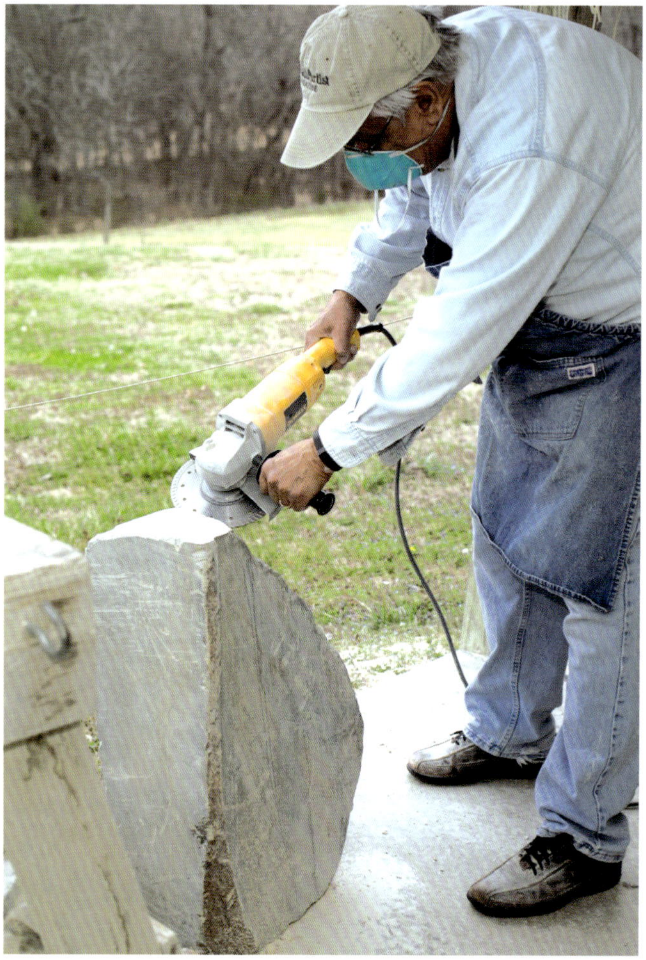

Eddie cutting stone for a new work of art

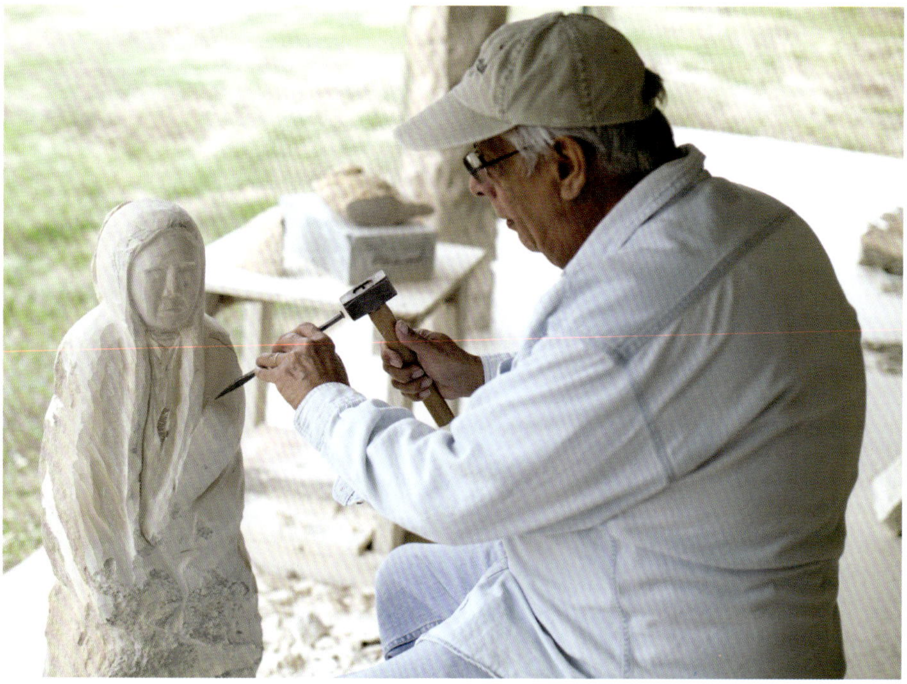

Eddie carving a Cherokee maiden from limestone

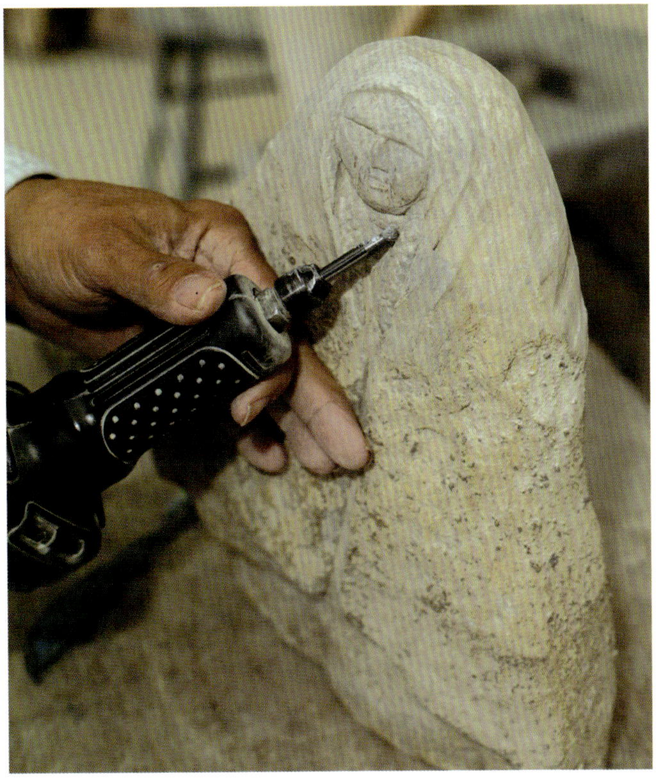

Eddie working on a carving of a Native American, in limestone

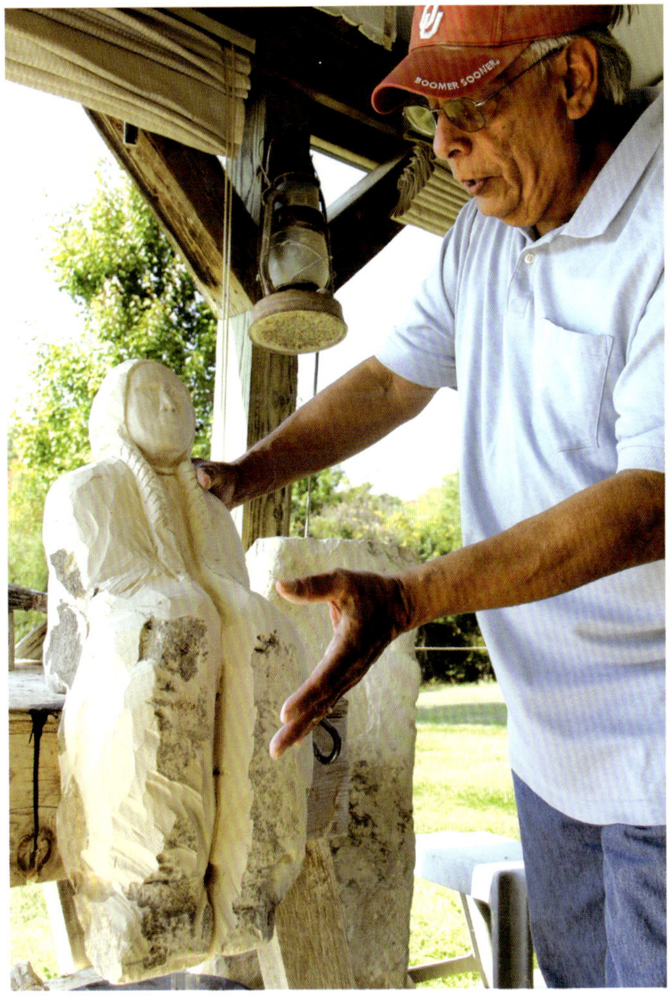

Eddie examining a limestone piece in progress

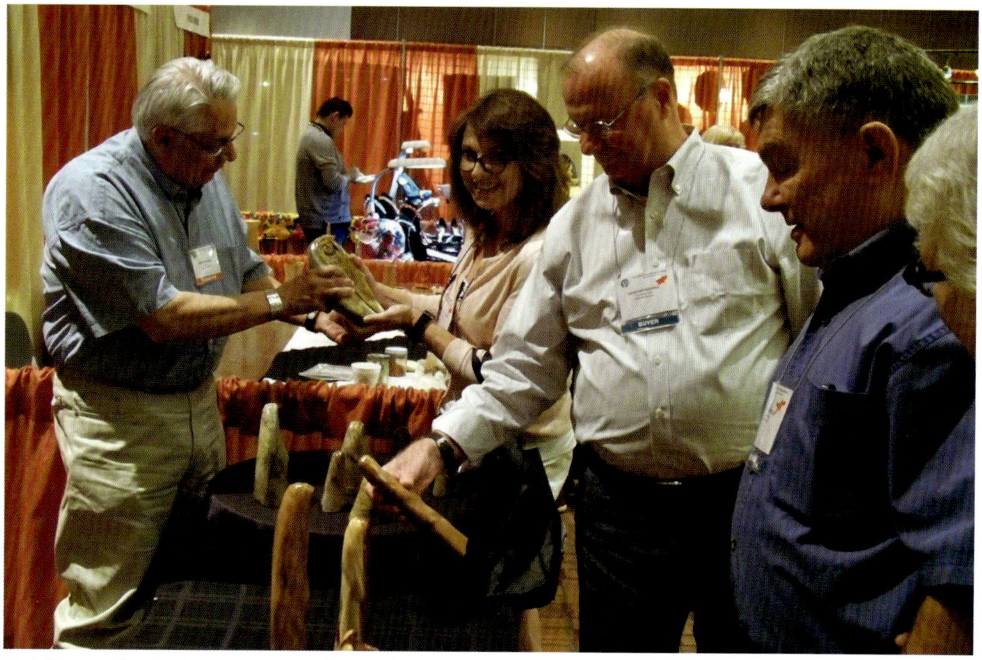

Eddie at the Indian Arts and Crafts Association show in Albuquerque, New Mexico.

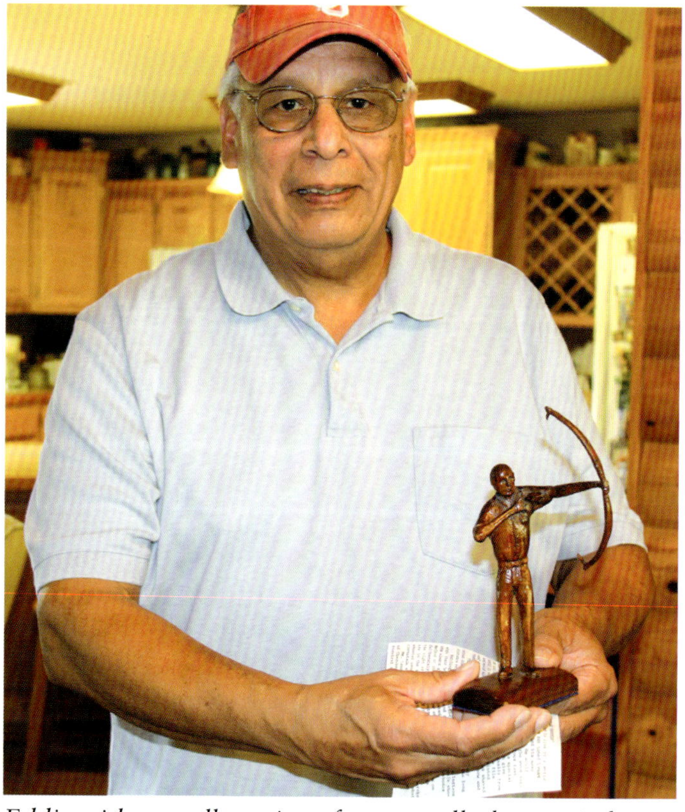

Eddie with a small carving of a cornstalk shooter, in honor of Lyman Vann (Photograph by Jamie Murphy, *Cherokee Phoenix*)

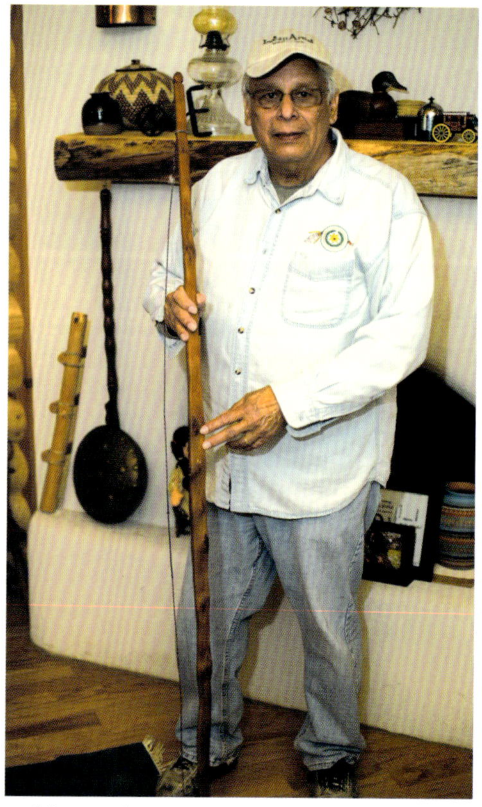

Eddie with a primitive bois d'arc wood bow given to him by a Cherokee artisan (Photograph by Brandon Scott)

Chapter Ten

Reflections

There are times when Eddie likes to sit back and reflect on his career—where he came from and how he made it to where he is today—and connect once again with the mystical sense of destiny that has been his guide along the way. Much like the great Indian artists who came before him, Eddie knows he is on a journey that has crossed the generations as he seeks to keep Cherokee myths, legends, and culture alive. Myths about the earth, animals, and nature are very important to Cherokees. "Indians have a story for nearly everything—the *Great Mystic Hawk, How the Opossum Got His Tail, The Ice Man and the Fire* and *The Legend of Red Cedar Wood* and why it is red. I have done carvings of many of these legends."[1]

The Cherokees, like other Native Americans, believe in one Supreme Being, not spirits and idols. They developed myths over thousands of years and passed them down orally to teach life lessons to the young. Cherokees with special lineages were chosen to communicate these traditions.

Eddie takes great satisfaction in carving tales such as *The Ice Man and the Fire* in wood and stone for his Cherokee people. So said the *Wichita Eagle's* in-depth story on him and his work. This legend tells how the Cherokees found a great lake after a terrible fire. Here is the story that Eddie's elders passed on to him.

> Once a tribe of Cherokees was burning the woods when a poplar tree caught fire and burned into the ground until a great hole formed. The fire kept burning and the people did not know what to do.
>
> Seven messengers were sent to visit a little man in a house of ice. The messengers found the little man, who wore his hair in two long braids that hung to the ground. They asked him if he could help put out the fire.
>
> He agreed and unplaited his long hair, took it up in one hand and slapped it across the palm of his other hand. A gust of wind rushed past the messengers. He slapped the hair across his hand again, and a light rain began to fall. The third time he did it, sleet mixed with rain, and the last time he slapped his hair against his open hand, hailstones fell to the ground. He told the messengers to return home.

The next morning, the people were watching the fire when a wind began to blow. The rain fell, then sleet; steam rose from the fire. Finally, hail fell on the great fire, and steam and smoke rose from the collision of fire and ice. When the fire was extinguished, the people looked into the hole and found a great lake where the burning pit had been.[2]

The newspaper pointed out that Eddie had heard the story when he was a young man and held it in the back of his mind for years. It resurfaced when he found a large chunk of alabaster in New Mexico and decided to begin the carving.

It took Eddie six months to carve and polish *The Ice Man and the Fire*. He said he never knew the exact significance of the story but believed somewhere down deep in the green and gray alabaster, the stone itself had a story to tell.

"Morrison carves wood and stone but there's more to his work," the newspaper reported. "He also carves stories. They are stories of his Cherokee people and stories he thinks the stone and wood want to tell."

Although Eddie said *The Ice Man and the Fire* piece is worth a lot of money, he decided to keep it in his private collection. "There are a few pieces that I've kept for myself because I think it's good to hold on to your work, to live with it. I feel blessed that I sell most of my work, but it's important to keep some to pass on to my family."[3] The sculpture is now on display at the Cherokee Nation Veterans Center at the Cherokee Nation tribal complex.

"Like the stories passed to him by his elders, Morrison will one day pass on his stories to his children and their children," the *Eagle* pointed out.

Some of Eddie's admirers believe there is a touch of the miraculous in his work, and at times he wonders if that is true. "I don't know about the miraculous, but I do know that art is a passion within me, a gift from the Creator, and it won't go away. . . . I still get a thrill when one of my carvings or sculptures is completed. I'm just in awe of what I have done."[4]

One day, Eddie realized that his work, indeed, flows from him naturally. "It was not so in the beginning, but today I can visualize what the finished piece will look like. Then that concept goes through my hands on a piece of wood or stone."

Like great singers, composers, or painters, Eddie is one of those people who feels he was born to create. "I make art because it's in my blood, I guess, and the good Lord blessed me with a gift. I want to keep doing stone sculpturing as long as I can."[5]

But Eddie is quick to point out that his artistic skills were not developed overnight. "It takes a lot of hard work and hours and hours of honing the skills one may have and a lot of trial and error and being willing to move forward."

Through the years Eddie has come to believe that art is an intuitive sort of thing—what some might call "looking at the clouds"—but he says it's more than that. "I will have an idea and will think about it long and hard until it germinates in my mind and I know exactly what to do to turn it into a beautiful work of art."

According to Eddie, there is a fine distinction between working with wood and working with stone. "With the wood, you can pretty well see the form. With stone, you have to think a little differently and have a design in mind before you start. Generally I can see the image in my mind and have a good idea of what will fit in the stone. Sometimes I have to sketch it out on paper but only if I don't have a clear picture of what I want to do."[6]

Eddie's love for nature and the works of nature are clearly visible in his art. He considers the natural forms of the wood and stone and believes in letting the materials speak for themselves, for he believes that they have their own stories to tell.

That philosophy influences every area of his work, and sometimes he jokingly compares his own life to his art. "My life has been like one of the wood or stone pieces I carve. I've chipped away all the rough stuff and all I have today is what I have become."

Those who observe his beautiful works often ask him where he gets his inspiration. He answers that when he began the journey, he read a lot of books about the myths and legends of Native Americans. He learned much about the Hopis, Pueblos, Navajos, Apaches, and others. But, of course, the myths and legends of the Cherokees have always been his main interest.

Today he follows a formula that gives him a lot of stability in his work. "First, I nurture the concept in my head and the different themes I want to follow. Then I try to work from nature with wood and stone and follow the natural lines I see in them."

The great iconic painter and sculptor Michelangelo, whose works Eddie greatly admires, once said of a piece of stone, "There's an image in there waiting to come out." Eddie tries to remember that, for he knows it is true.

Eddie has a great respect for Michelangelo, Rodin, and Bernini and the Greek, Roman, and Egyptian sculptors of ancient times. "What amazes me is the kind of tools they used. I use modern-day power tools and instruments but some of those artists had to use stone tools. And their works were monumental in size. I look at them in awe and it's difficult for me to fathom how they did it."

A smile creased his face when he mentioned the monumental sculptures on Mount Rushmore. "Sometimes I wonder why there is no Native American image beside Washington, Jefferson, Lincoln, and Roosevelt. I understand they are doing a stone carving of Chief Crazy Horse in the Black Hills of South Dakota and, of course, he was an Oglala Sioux chieftain."

Some of Eddie's sculptures depict an Indian wearing a wolf skin, feathers, or blanket. "These are some of my favorites for I love tradition and the history of our people." He also carves animals that are prominent in Indian lore, particularly bears, eagles, and buffalos.

Even after all these years and his remarkable success, Eddie wants to branch out in his work. "There are different stages in your career; you think differently and you want to grow and you want your art to grow so you can share something different and more exciting than anything you have ever done before."

There are good ideas everywhere, and Eddie tries to take advantage of them. "I want to translate those ideas into masterful works of art. Take cornstalk shooting, for instance; I could do a whole series of sculptures on cornstalk shooting."

Recently he started thinking about how his grandmother and aunts wore colorful scarves wrapped around their heads. He wants to do a whole series of figures of Cherokee Indian women wearing those headscarves.

Eddie said that wherever he goes, people always ask how long it takes him to complete a woodcarving or stone sculpture. His answer is simple: "It takes me as long as I want to take. It depends on whether it is a complicated piece or a simple one. I always know there's an endpoint but until I reach that point, it's not finished."

It is not unusual for Eddie to work on four or five pieces at a time. "Sometimes when I'm working on a certain piece in my studio, I'll get a mental block; my mind just goes blank. So I put it aside and work on another piece or two others for awhile."

After a time, a new vision spurs and whips his tired mind into action. "Then, all of a sudden, I go back to the first piece and know exactly what I want to do to finish it."

Eddie sometimes marvels at his profession. "It's so great when I get a concept and I see it come alive before my eyes. For instance, I take an old piece of dead wood or a common rock that looks like nothing but I see something in it and my work brings life back to the wood and rock. It gives me a thrill to see something come out of nothing."

In north-central Kansas, about three million acres are covered with fence posts made by Kansas settlers from a single bed of rock. The area is known as "Land of the Post Rock." When Eddie first saw these acres and acres of limestone fence posts, he knew that the stone had a life of its own. "It was created millions of years ago and, over the eons, collected fossils. When early-day settlers came to Kansas, they didn't have trees to cut for fence posts so they cut the limestone posts. Then a hundred years later I come along, see the potential in the posts, buy them, and make something beautiful out of them."

As he looks back on his career, he is thankful for what his art has meant in his life. "Art has taken me to a lot of places I've never been before and my art has gone around the world. And that's really something for a poor boy who grew up on Ward Street in Tahlequah who lived with his elderly grandmother."[7]

Eddie admitted that at times it feels strange knowing that people in other countries like his artwork and purchase it for their homes and offices. "Actually, it's a great feeling when anyone, wherever they live, comes along and purchases one of my carvings or sculptures. What an honor for them to take the piece to their homes, businesses, or a museum. That's the greatest honor an artist can have."[8]

Although Eddie had great success in art shows all across America, he decided to cut back to only five per year. "For years I did eight shows each year, some of the biggest and best in America. But I came to the conclusion that was too many. I would always have to return home and work on more carvings and sculptures to get ready for the next show."

One reason why he decided to cut back was because he felt he was rushing his work. "Buyers can always tell if your work was done in a big hurry. Indian art is a big business and these buyers have keen eyes."

The sale of his works of art brings Eddie a lot of satisfaction that is more spiritual than financial. The Cherokee Nation has purchased a number of his works, including a woodcarving called *Trail of Tears*, which had been in his personal collection for twenty-five years.

•••

Eddie will tell everyone that there is no way for him to describe how much he loves his work. "When you are away from the work that you love, even for a short time, you say, 'Man, I need to get back in the studio and get back to work.'"

There is a fire in his spirit to keep Cherokee culture alive. "We Cherokees should be proud of who we are and what we have today. We came over the Trail of Tears, where thousands of our ancestors died in one of the most tragic events in the history of this land. But Cherokees were brave and strong of heart. They were able to break every chain that has shackled them in the past and our people looked to the future with hope in their hearts. And look at where we are today—a thriving people and the biggest tribe in America with more than 330,000 on the official rolls and a million or maybe two million more with Cherokee blood. I like what former Chief Wilma Mankiller once said, 'If you have one drop of Cherokee blood, you are Cherokee.'"

All of his life, Eddie has been convinced that there's something special about the Cherokee people and all Native Americans. "We were the first ones to settle this great land and have survived for hundreds of years."

Like most other Cherokees, Eddie wishes he knew more about the lost history of his ancestors, for he would like to pay tribute to them with his art. "I've often wondered about our ancestors and wish I could journey back in history before the Europeans landed in this land and learn about my people's customs and legends and learn the truth that has been lost in mystery. That would be so very exciting."

He tries to imagine the Cherokee culture during the time before the Europeans arrived. "How did they approach life? Where did they come from and how far? What was their belief system and what influenced that belief system? How did they dress and did they dress differently for each season of the year? What was their family life like? I would like to have answers to all of these questions for if I knew more about their lives back then, perhaps I could bring that era to life with my carvings and sculptures."

Although mystery shrouds the life and times of the historic Cherokees, Eddie believes they were a prosperous, peace-loving people. "All we can do now is make our own suppositions of how they really looked and thought, and what their life was like. We probably would be surprised how wrong the so-called experts are when we read their interpretations of that era. All we can do is just guess. In our day, all we know is what has been written about them by the Europeans along with their interpretation of Cherokee life back then. I wish I knew what life was like 500 years before the explorers came to this land."

Pride wells up in Eddie's heart when he remembers all of the great Cherokee leaders who blazed a path for the magnificent Cherokee people. Their roots trace back through genealogical evidence to the great chief Austenaco, who lived in the 1700s. In the year 1762, Austenaco and two other chiefs—Outracite and Uschesees—traveled to England in a British man-of-war frigate to strengthen their tribe's friendship with King George III. They are known in Cherokee history as "Emissaries of Peace." While in England, they visited the Tower of London and Buckingham Palace and had an audience with King George. A famous painting entitled *Emissaries of Peace* hangs in the office of the principal chief of the Cherokee Nation.

Eddie also knows that that there is a long line of heroic Cherokee leaders who dreamed dreams of a brighter tomorrow for their people, such as Chief John Ross, the statesman who led his people over the Trail of Tears to Indian Territory, and Elias Boudinot, the erudite journalist who became founder and editor of the *Cherokee Phoenix*, the Cherokees' first newspaper. "Of course, there was Sequoyah, the great scholar who gave us our brilliant syllabary, and Stand Watie, the warrior soldier, and hundreds of others. All of these great men have left a profound impact on my life."

Will Rogers is a more modern influence on Eddie. "He is everyone's favorite. I liked him because he was proud to tell people he was Cherokee."

Some of Eddie's admirers have asked him how the creative process works in his life. "It's very difficult to describe for, at times, it is somewhat of a mystical experience . . . I get lost in time and find myself oblivious to everything that is going on around me. Yes, It's very mystical."

Someone visiting Eddie's studio in Steely Hollow on any workday will find him wearing heavy gloves to protect his wrists as he, chisel in hand, leans over a large piece of limestone and meticulously chips away an oval face with high cheekbones in the natural lines of the rock. And the visitor senses that a beautiful carving is not far away.

Eddie says there are three types of finishing for different materials. "The most tedious is probably the wood, because I use a hand-rub finish. You rub a mixture of oils and varnishes into the wood, and it penetrates the wood. There's about seven or eight hand-rubbed coats. You have to let it dry twenty-four hours between each coat and lightly sand to get it.

"The more coats you put on it, the more gloss you get on the piece of wood. It's more tedious to use, but it's better than polyurethane or anything like that. It looks natural."[9]

Working with alabaster is different. "You have to use what you call an alabaster compound and buff it into the stone. Then you polish it . . . and then you put a protective coat in it if you want to get a real high shine."

Eddie does not polish his works of art if they are to be displayed outside, especially the limestone. "That's something that won't take a real high gloss on it, but the wood pieces and the alabaster and the marble, I will polish."

Beautiful color variations in the wood Eddie works with have always fascinated him. "They are visible in the cedar wood I use and allow the gentle curves or unusual twists naturally found in the wood to appear in the finished pieces. When I finish it, I sit back and look at it and it sends chills down my spine."

Eddie believes that red cedar is not necessarily an exotic wood, but it has a character all its own and he has learned a lot while working with it. For instance, if he sees that the piece of cedar has some defect, he relates it to people. "A person can have a defect in one area, but they still have another beauty that shines through."[10]

The wood doesn't have to be perfect—just as most people are not perfect—but Eddie said that doesn't matter to him. "You see a lot of people that might have a handicap, and some of them are just real beautiful people, too."

Eddie uses silver and turquoise in some of his wood pieces, and he believes they complement one another. "The people really like it and it adds another dimension to my work."

Some have asked him about the source of his artistic skills, but he knows there is no easy answer. "My skill is a mystery to me. I don't know where it came from other than to say it is a gift given to me by the great Creator. I'm glad it has been given to me and I know I must use it wisely."

Eddie realizes he is no Indian prodigy like some of the great painters and sculptors of history. "But I get the same thrill they must have enjoyed when I see my work take form and substance." After each work is completed, he gives thanks to the Creator.

Some of his works enchant him more than others. For instance, one of his favorites is a woodcarving that is on display in Caldwell at the Border Queen Museum. "It's a picture of an old Western town with cattle running through the streets and cowboys on horses. I carved Native Americans in the four corners of the picture watching the herds of cattle and cowboys taking over the land."

Some compare Eddie's work to that of Allan Houser, which he considers a real compliment. "They say we have the same motif and style. But that is not true. Although it is a great honor to be so compared, no one compares to Houser. If you look closely at his work and mine, there is a world of difference. I do not feel that any of my art is great enough to be compared to the master sculptors of ages past or that of my mentor Allan Houser. All I can do is keep trying to stand in their shadows."

There are sculptors from many other tribes at the art shows Eddie attends. "There are Hopis and Navajos, Pueblos and Apaches and others. I enjoy getting acquainted with them and observing their work. Some have become good friends and I have learned a lot from them."

Eddie's hobby is collecting art from his fellow artists. He considers their paintings, sculptures, pottery, and native jewelry great artistic treasures.

Eddie is proud to be a Cherokee. "There's something about the Cherokee people that makes them want to get up every time they are knocked down. The removal and Trail of Tears could have been the end of us as a nation. But we were determined to survive and we did."

Eddie believes that education had a lot to do with the Cherokee rise from the ashes. "We've always believed in education. We also had our own government and believed in the rule of law."

Sometimes Eddie wonders what the Cherokee people would be like today if the Presbyterian, Baptist, and Methodist missionaries had not brought Christianity to them. "I'm not exactly sure what we would be worshipping today. Most all Native Americans believe in one God and Cherokees in general are very religious. Today there are Indian Baptist and Methodist churches everywhere and a few Presbyterian."

Eddie thinks a lot about his future. "The real heavy stone work takes a toll on your body. You have to be able to lift it and turn it and it's tough physical work. Some of the pieces weigh as much as 400 pounds and others much more than that. Maybe I'll do a few paintings or start doing wax carvings and then on to bronze. Bronze is very popular today and I think I would enjoy it. But whatever I do, it will be about Indians."

Eddie loves going to the art shows. "I used to say, 'Boy, I hope someday if I ever get real well known or make enough money, I can quit doing the shows.'" However, he says he will never stop going to the shows, where he meets old friends and so many new people and sells his work.

"I told Faye, 'I don't know how much longer we can keep doing this.' 'Well, as long as we're having fun, we'll keep doing it,' she said."

There may be a major work of art in Eddie's future. "There's always that one thing you would like to leave as a legacy. I keep thinking about the Cherokee people and where they came from and where they are today and I would like to tie all that together and depict it in some three-dimensional form. It will be a large piece and I've thought about setting it on a hillside somewhere—perhaps on a well-traveled road—for thousands of people to see and enjoy and take pictures."

He continued, "I have been truly blessed . . . that people have enjoyed my work. I have different collectors all across the country that come back year after year to purchase my pieces and it really makes me feel good that they still like my work. Sometimes, people will come up to me at a show and say, 'I bought some of your work years ago.'"

Eddie looks into the future and prays that the Cherokee people will keep hope alive.

Epilogue

A Vision of Hope

Eddie and Faye's hilltop home in Steely Hollow nestles in a range of hills and deep ravines near a small but beautiful lake. It stands like a guardian angel looking down on the fertile valley below. A visitor to their beautiful log home—semi-secluded and surrounded by heavy woods—will find a calm retreat and place of inspiration. In autumn he will marvel at the lovely colors and the early-morning sun that raises the veil on the horizon, milky blue where the sky meets the earth. In spring he will see deer and wild turkeys roaming the woods and meadows in the valley below and young plants pushing their way through the soil in search of the sun. He will hear the music of nature as the wind murmurs through the hills under a ceaselessly changing sky.

Heaven seems a little closer and the clock moves a little slower on the hill where they live, and there's something about it that makes one want to whisper. When the visitor gets to know them better, he senses that Eddie and Faye have found great contentment in the woods in Steely Hollow.

Although people often ask Eddie when he is going to retire, he has no plans to ride off into the sunset like the Lone Ranger and Tonto. Rather, he is quick to respond that an artist never really retires. "I'm going to continue working as long as I'm physically able. I'll always be happy creating works of art for others to enjoy."

More than anything else, Eddie wants to be faithful to Cherokee traditions and culture and desires to make those traditions burn like a fire in the lives of Cherokees. "May they always remember who they are, where they came from, and always be proud of their heritage. My life will be complete if I, even in some small way, can do my part to keep that heritage alive."

The prayer of his heart for his Cherokee brothers and sisters is that they will listen to the voices of the past—their ancestors—and hear the lessons they are trying to teach them. He also encourages them to listen to the voices of the future and recognize the sounds of their calling, telling them the kind of people they are destined to become. And finally, he says his people must listen to the present, to the voices within them and the voices of those around them who have great wisdom. For then they will find their destiny.

Eddie explained it this way. "If we fail to listen, we will never learn, and if we fail to learn, we will never be able to fulfill our destiny and the bright future that is ours. The gate is open wide before us and the Cherokee people must march through it hand in hand as we go on to the greater glory that is just around the corner waiting for us."

More than anything else, Eddie wants to be faithful to his vision of hope for the Cherokees that, through the years, he has carried in his heart. It is the same vision he has shared through his paintings, carvings, and sculptures and will continue to share today, tomorrow, and far into the future.

Appendix A

Masterworks

Eddie Morrison's heart leaps when a new idea for a piece of art flashes through his mind. He can hardly wait to get to his studio to choose the wood or stone that will help him bring his vision to life. Then the vision makes its way through his hands and onto the carving and into a beautiful work of art.

There is a mystical and reverential dimension in Eddie's work born out of his respect for the red cedar, Kansas limestone, Colorado Yule Marble, New Mexico alabaster, and other wood and stone that find their way into his studio. There he will create something of artistic beauty that will capture the hearts, minds, and imaginations of people everywhere who will see and admire his work.

No boundaries or parameters confine Eddie to the genres of those who have gone before him or his fellow artists today. His work spans a wide spectrum of themes that takes him from a very simple woodcarving to a quite complex stone carving that requires months of work. His subjects include myths and legends, historical events, monuments to great Cherokee men and women, the elements—wind, earth, and fire—Cherokee Thanksgiving, animals, ancient Cherokees and ancestors, and a hundred others that challenge his amazing skill and passion.

Eddie takes great pride in each of his creations. "I try to make the pieces dignified with a lot of integrity. At times you will see pictures of Native Americans sad and downtrodden. I try to give them dignity, especially on their faces, for we are survivors and I want to celebrate our survival."[1]

Eddie has created hundreds of works of art that have found their way into galleries and private homes around the world. Observers will notice a predominance of female figures, which come from his grandmother's influence on his life.

He also enjoys creating works featuring bears and buffalos. "I love doing bears, and people love to collect my bear carvings. I've made so many, I've lost count and made them out of all kinds of materials: stone, wood, and clay. Cherokees wore bearskins to keep them warm and they also thought the skins imparted strength to them. And I like to depict buffalos and wolves. The Cherokee Nation now has its own herd of buffalos up near Grove, Oklahoma, and the Cherokees once had a buffalo dance ceremony. And wolves play an important role in Cherokee history."

Some of Eddie's works are historical in nature, such as *Keeper of the Fire*. This refers to a flame the Cherokees carried with them over the Trail of Tears to Indian Territory and a sacred dance performed around it called the Stomp Dance. There are several Stomp Dance grounds in the Cherokee Nation.

A keeper of the fire builds the fire at dawn on the day of the dance and keeps it burning into the night. The dance includes at least one "shell shaker" wearing leg rattles, usually made of turtle shells filled with pebbles. The ceremonial leaders make sacrifices, pray, take medicine, cleanse in water, and smoke the pipe. The dance goes on far into the night. The purpose of the Stomp Dance is to worship God. Even though Cherokees belong to several different denominations, many traditional Cherokees participate in Stomp Dances.

Here are some of Eddie's favorite works.

Indian Stick Ball Player, a pen-and-ink

Young Cherokee boy shooting a squirrel with a blowgun, a pen-and-ink

A Promise for as Long as the Grass Grows, a carving in relief

Our Children Are Our Children—Eddie said, "This piece represents a mother and child and our feeling for keeping them in the family and the child being raised traditionally and not adopted outside the native nation"

Indian warrior with a wolf cape over his head

Those Who Came Before, a 1,600-pound piece in Kansas limestone located on the old Chisholm Trail on the border between Oklahoma and Kansas

The Ice Man and the Fire, a piece in New Mexico alabaster located in the Cherokee Nation Veterans Center

Beautiful Indian maiden wearing a headscarf, a carving in Kansas limestone

Blessings, a person holding an eagle feather, which is sacred to Cherokees, giving thanks for every blessing

Man walking with a staff, woman holding a piece of bread, and boy carrying a dog

Thanksgiving, a carving in stone of a woman holding a piece of pottery

Cherokee man with long braids holding an eagle feather

Ancient Cherokee man with a topknot and feathers going down his back

The noble buffalo, once the centerpiece for the Cherokee buffalo dance

Indian wearing bearskin for protection and to draw the creature's strength

Man wearing a cape blowing in the wind

Indian lady, a carving in red cedar inlaid with turquoise all around

Ancient Fire Keeper, with topknot, tending to the flames

Two eagles, important symbols for Cherokees and all Native Americans

I'll Race You to the Top, with two small bears climbing up a rock, representing Indian achievements

Serenity, a Cherokee in a quiet place contemplating the meaning of life

Indian mother and her daughter, searching for the courage to go through life

Stand by Me, a cedar carving of a man and woman on a marble base

Survivors of the Trail of Tears, with an oversize Cherokee woman lying on the ground watching miniatures of her people as they march through many hardships on their way to Indian Territory

Cherokee grandmother holding a child close to her heart with a blanket wrapped securely around her

The Oklahoma Land Run of 1889, with people on horseback running for the land that the government was giving away, and four Indians watching them take their land away

Cherokee Pow Wow Eagle Dancer, a pen-and-ink

Cherokee man giving thanks for a basket of herbs he is holding

Appendix B

Galleries and Shows

Following is a partial list of shows that Eddie has attended as well as places where his works have been displayed. There are many others.

National Museum of the American Indian—Smithsonian,	Washington, D.C.
Adobe Artes Gallery	Long Island, New York
Museum of Contemporary Native Arts	Santa Fe, New Mexico
National Museum of the American Indian	New York City
Denver Botanic Gardens	Denver, Colorado
Autry Museum	Los Angeles, California
Khot La Cha Gallery	Vancouver, Canada
Santa Fe Indian Market	Santa Fe, New Mexico
Wichita Indian Museum	Wichita, Kansas
University of Kansas	Lawrence, Kansas
Haskell University Indian Market	Lawrence, Kansas
American Indian Center	Abilene, Kansas
Turquoise Gallery	Austin, Texas
Indian Arts and Crafts Association	Albuquerque, New Mexico
Indian Arts and Crafts Association	Phoenix, Arizona
Eiteljorg Museum	Indianapolis, Indiana
Cahokia Mounds Museum	Collinsville, Illinois
Milwaukee Indian Summer Festival	Milwaukee, Wisconsin
Angel Mounds Museum	Evansville, Indiana
Asheville Indian Market	Asheville, North Carolina
Indian Craft Shop—Department of the Interior	Washington, D.C.
Tesoro Cultural Foundation Indian Market	Morrison, Colorado
Trail of Tears Art Show	Tahlequah, Oklahoma
Five Civilized Tribes Museum	Muskogee, Oklahoma
Cherokee National Holiday Show	Tahlequah, Oklahoma

Cherokee Arts Center	Tahlequah, Oklahoma
Cherokee Art Market	Tulsa, Oklahoma
Indian Summer Festival	Bartlesville, Oklahoma
Tulsa Indian Market	Tulsa, Oklahoma
Philbrook Museum of Art	Tulsa, Oklahoma
Gilcrease Museum	Tulsa, Oklahoma
Heard Museum	Phoenix, Arizona
Pueblo Grande Museum	Phoenix, Arizona

Appendix C

Recognitions and Demonstrations

Recognitions

Faculty Department Award for Outstanding Student in Three-Dimensional Arts, Institute of American Indian Arts, Santa Fe, New Mexico

The Eagle carving displayed in the Office of the Secretary of the Interior, Washington, D.C.

Artist of the Month, Indian Craft Shop, Washington, D.C.

Strength of Life design chosen for the first official Christmas ornament produced by the Cherokee Nation

The Ice Man and the Fire on display in the Cherokee Nation Veterans Center, Tahlequah, Oklahoma

Artist in Residence, Denver Botanic Gardens, Denver, Colorado

Demonstrations

Wellington High School Gifted Class, Wellington, Kansas

Milwaukee Indian Summer Festival Carving Demonstration, Milwaukee, Wisconsin

Adobe Artes Gallery, Long Island, New York

Indian Craft Shop, Department of the Interior, Washington, D.C.

National Museum of the American Indian Cherokee Days, Washington, D.C.

Selected Art Show Awards

From the Santa Fe Indian Market, Santa Fe, New Mexico

From the Eiteljorg Museum, Indianapolis, Indiana

From the Indian Arts and Crafts Association, Albuquerque, New Mexico
From the Tesoro Cultural Foundation Indian Market, Morrison, Colorado
From the Trail of Tears Art Show, Tahlequah, Oklahoma
From the Five Civilized Tribes Museum, Muskogee, Oklahoma
From the Tulsa Indian Market, Tulsa, Oklahoma

Notes

Chapter One

1. Eddie Morrison, interview by the author, Cherokee County, Oklahoma, November 3, 2014.
2. Ibid.
3. Ibid.
4. Faye Morrison, interview by the author, Cherokee County, Oklahoma, December 1, 2014.
5. Eddie Morrison interview.

Chapter Two

1. Eddie Morrison interview.
2. Ibid.
3. Ibid.
4. Ibid.
5. Nancy Hummingbird, interview by the author, Tulsa, Oklahoma, February 13, 2015.
6. Ibid.
7. Eddie Morrison interview.
8. Ibid.
9. Jesse Hummingbird, interview by the author, Bisbee, Arizona, February 11, 2015.
10. Ibid.
11. Ibid.
12. Eddie Morrison interview.

Chapter Three

1. James Locke, correspondence to the author, Langley, Oklahoma, December 8, 2014.
2. Ibid.
3. Ibid.

4. Ibid.

5. Dwain Denny, interview by the author, Tahlequah, Oklahoma, December 2, 2014.

6. Eddie Morrison interview.

7. Isabel Baker, correspondence to the author, Tahlequah, Oklahoma, November 18, 2014.

8. Ibid.

9. Eddie Morrison interview.

10. Eddie Morrison, interview by Julie Pearson-Little Thunder, Oklahoma State University, Stillwater, Oklahoma, September 20, 2013.

11. Eddie Morrison, interview by the author.

12. Faye Morrison interview.

13. Eddie Morrison, interview by the author.

14. Ibid.

15. Ibid.

16. Ibid.

Chapter Four

1. Eddie Morrison, interview by the author.

2. Ibid.

3. Ibid.

4. Ibid.

5. Ibid.

6. Eddie Morrison, interview by Pearson-Little Thunder.

7. Renee Fite, "Artist Relies on Spirituality," *Tahlequah Daily Press*, December 31, 2012.

8. Eddie Morrison, interview by the author.

9. Ibid.

10. Phyllis Griekspoor, *Wichita Eagle*, May 18, 1997.

Chapter Five

1. Griekspoor.

2. Ibid.

3. Ibid.

4. Ibid.

5. Ibid.

6. Ibid.

7. Eddie Morrison, interview by the author.

8. Griekspoor.

9. Eddie Morrison, interview by the author.

10. Ibid.

11. Faye Morrison interview.

Chapter Six

1. Eddie Morrison, interview by the author.

2. Eddie Morrison, interview by Pearson-Little Thunder.

Chapter Seven

1. Jennifer Morrison Barker, correspondence to the author, Wellington, Kansas, January 6, 2015.

2. Jesse Hummingbird interview.

3. Monica Morrison Glass, correspondence to the author, December 5, 2014.

Chapter Eight

1. Jami Murphy, "Cherokee Finds, Maintains Passion for Sculpting," *Cherokee Phoenix*, November 7, 2014.

2. Julie Hubbard, "Tahlequah Sculptor Displays Work Across Country," *Muskogee Phoenix,* December 1, 2002.

3. Hubbard.

4. Eddie Morrison, interview by the author.

5. Eddie Morrison, interview by Pearson-Little Thunder.

6. Eddie Morrison, interview by the author.

Chapter Nine

1. Hubbard.

2. Donna Tinnin, correspondence to the author, Tahlequah, Oklahoma, December 5, 2014.

3. Callie Chunestudy, correspondence to the author, Tahlequah, Oklahoma, December 9, 2014.

4. Jane Osti, interview by the author, Tahlequah, Oklahoma, January 6, 2015.

5. Victoria Vasquez, correspondence to the author, November 19, 2014.

6. Brett Greenwood, "Sculpting Heritages," *Tulsa Voice,* October 1-4, 2014.

7. Buddy McCarty, correspondence to the author, December 18, 2014.

8. Baker correspondence.

Chapter Ten

1. Tara McClain, "Revisiting Stories," *Wichita Eagle,* July 9, 2000.

2. Ibid.

3. Fite.

4. McClain.

5. Fite.

6. Eddie Morrison, interview by the author.
7. Fite.
8. Eddie Morrison, interview by the author.
9. Hubbard.
10. Eddie Morrison, interview by Pearson-Little Thunder.

Appendix A

1. Eddie Morrison, interview by the author.